If Mama Ain't Happy reads like a lette⟨...⟩ friend who knows you inside and out ⟨...⟩ Rachel share her inspiring journey fro⟨...⟩ ⟨...⟩ into grace, but her new take on rules as "life-giving, not life-sucking" will put the wind at your back.

SANDRA R. BLACKARD, mom of two, author of *SAY WHAT YOU SEE®* for Parents and Teachers

An empowering and practical guide that encourages mothers to set boundaries at home, strengthen their faith, and enjoy the ride.

JENNIFER L. SCOTT, mom of four, *New York Times* bestselling author of *Lessons from Madame Chic*

I love Rachel and her deep momma wisdom. As a mom of nine, I know caring for myself helps me love my children well.

JAMERRILL STEWART, mom of nine, LargeFamilyTable.com

Rachel Norman is my favorite parenting expert by far. Her down-to-earth style and humorous perspective are a breath of fresh air!

ANNA GEIGER, mom of six, The Measured Mom

Finally someone is telling the truth about motherhood. This is the most authentic, commonsense guide to motherhood I've read. You'll find yourself nodding and laughing the whole way through.

LAUREN TAMM, mom of two, The Military Wife and Mom

If Mama Ain't Happy

If Mama Ain't Happy

Why minding healthy boundaries is good for your whole family

Rachel Norman

TYNDALE
MOMENTUM®

A Tyndale nonfiction imprint

Visit Tyndale online at tyndale.com.

Visit Tyndale Momentum online at tyndalemomentum.com.

Visit Rachel Norman at amotherfarfromhome.com.

Tyndale, Tyndale's quill logo, *Tyndale Momentum*, and the Tyndale Momentum logo are registered trademarks of Tyndale House Ministries. Tyndale Momentum is a nonfiction imprint of Tyndale House Publishers, Carol Stream, Illinois.

If Mama Ain't Happy: Why Minding Healthy Boundaries Is Good for Your Whole Family

Designed by Jacqueline L. Nuñez

Published in association with the literary agency of William K. Jensen Literary Agency, 119 Bampton Court, Eugene, Oregon 97404.

For information about special discounts for bulk purchases, please contact Tyndale House Publishers at csresponse@tyndale.com, or call 1-855-277-9400.

Library of Congress Cataloging-in-Publication Data

A catalog record for this book is available from the Library of Congress.

ISBN 978-1-4964-5980-0

Printed in the United States of America

28 27 26 25 24 23 22

7 6 5 4 3 2 1

*I am fully convinced, my dear brothers and sisters, that you are full of goodness. You know these things so well you can teach each other all about them. Even so, **I have been bold enough to write about some of these points, knowing that all you need is this reminder.***

ROMANS 15:14-15, NLT, EMPHASIS MINE

* * *

To my precious children, Ella Kate, Judah, Fletcher, Owen, and Hobson, who make life worth living

Table of Contents

Beloved mama,

I see you juggling diaper changes, feedings, naps, bedtimes, drops-offs, and pickups like a pro. I know you count these things as precious and feel privileged to do them. On the outside, you look as if you're coping just fine. But on the inside, you feel like you're going haywire trying to figure out how to do everything right.

You may be perpetually stressed, strung out, and exhausted. You may not feel good enough, smart enough, or secure enough. One small thing—like an unexpected bill in the mail or a sudden change in the family schedule—may make your heart beat out of your chest and send you into a tailspin.

You have no margin for surprises, problems, or inconveniences.

You've put the weight of the world on your shoulders.

Occasionally someone will tell you to "show yourself some grace," and you look at them like they are a purple alien from another galaxy. Okay. Sure. Genius idea. More grace. I'll get right on that!

I see you because for years I propelled my family forward by the sheer will of my dominant personality. I figured winners never quit and quitters never win. But somewhere deep down, I knew I was losing. My insecurities, inadequacies, and self-judgment drove me at a pace I could not sustain.

I was living in a dark prison of best practices and "shoulds" that weren't even mentioned in the Bible. I was a slave to all sorts of things I felt I "needed" to be doing even when they made me stressed, depressed, anxious, and miserable.

It's exhausting even remembering that time.

Eventually, my wild and careening runaway train came to an obstacle in the tracks that forced it to stop, giving me a lot of time to rest and reflect. All those emotions I'd been burying and avoiding came out. Tear by tear, I unloaded years of baggage, and in those quiet moments God found me. Through various events, encounters, and circumstances, He healed my heart.

I began to see that I'd been operating in a black-or-white, win-or-lose world. Either I was busy or I was lazy. Either I was successful or I was a failure. Either I was right or I was wrong. I'd been following tons of "life rules" someone else made up. Rules about housekeeping, child-rearing, and friend-making.

Now I'm on another path. A more pleasant one with some shade and occasional benches. And since I'm not careening down a cliff, I can stop and smell the flowers. Maybe even have a picnic here or there. Same number of kids, same number of chores, same number of meals to cook every day. Minus all the heaviness.

And the unrelenting weight of misery.

Maybe you are reading this because you want to enjoy your family life more, instead of feeling worn out and weary before you've even gotten dressed in the morning. Or because you want to lay your head on your pillow at night without replaying all your mistakes.

Mama, I wrote this book for you.

It is possible to stop disliking your life. To craft a home life that doesn't make you anxious, depressed, and weary. I believe you can create a life, day in and day out, that doesn't make you want to run away and escape. And that by discovering and respecting your spiritual, mental, emotional, and physical boundaries, you can have a fruitful private world that isn't choked by the worries of this life.

There's no time like the present; let's get to it.

Rachel Norman

CHAPTER 1

Happy-Go-Lucky . . . or Not

One wintry Friday morning, I helped my five kids (all under age seven) put on coats and rain boots before loading them into our minivan for what I hoped would be a pleasant homeschooling field trip.

To be honest, I love my kids to pieces, but I didn't really love teaching them at home. Most days my heart nearly pounded out of my chest as I tried to help the older kids with their schoolwork while making sure the toddlers didn't destroy the house or run off into the woods. Every day I counted down the minutes until the school day was over. Somehow, it never occurred to me that I could stop homeschooling. I was subconsciously convinced that if I didn't shower my daughter and four sons with attention and care all day, they would not feel loved. To prevent them from having to deal with rejection issues later on, I could endure some daily misery, right?

Field trips, especially those where wild little ones could run around and make all the noise they wanted, offered occasional breaks. So on this Friday, a trip to the botanical gardens in Dothan, Alabama, was just the ticket. It sounded educational, and these kids needed some education. The hour-long drive from our home in Florida to the gardens in Alabama was filled with happy chatter, and we arrived at our destination in good spirits. But within moments of turning onto the tree-lined arboretum road, I couldn't believe my eyes. Other than a few evergreen trees and bushes, everything looked brown and dead. The kids, who weren't interested in botany anyway, spent most of the morning hopping along the wooden bridges and slides on the grounds. I posed them for some pictures in the tropical plant greenhouse so I could post them on Instagram—with a homeschool hashtag, of course. Then off we went to the indoor trampoline park.

When we arrived home hours later, the kids were tired out and I was in a mood. They didn't even complain when I peeled off their coats and walked them to their rooms for naps and rest time. But as soon as I closed their bedroom doors, I started navel-gazing. A good homeschool teacher would have known that most plants are actually dead in the winter and gardens are basically ugly when most of the plants are dead. A familiar dark and heavy cloud settled on my heart.

To put it mildly, I wasn't a happy mama.

A FACT OF LIFE

"If mama ain't happy, ain't nobody happy."

I used to think women said this as a threat to get what they want. Like if Mama is embarrassed by her kids throwing tantrums in the grocery store, everyone will be sorry. Or if she can't have a ladies' night out or get a mani/pedi once a month, her husband will regret it.

I thought "if mama ain't happy, ain't nobody happy" was a warning. Then I got married, lived in three different countries, had five kids in five years, and was blindsided by a devastating health diagnosis.

And that's when I learned what that phrase really means. It's not a threat; it's what we in the South refer to as "a fact of life." Nobody's happy if mama ain't happy because her attitude affects everyone around her. It's not a warning; it's just how it is. If mama is depressed, stressed, overwhelmed, exhausted, frustrated, or irritable, everyone in the home feels it.

And when mom is relaxed, at peace, and content with herself and her life, everyone in the home benefits. She is more patient, kind, and present with those she loves. A happy mom lives her life without constantly trying to escape it.

> Nobody's happy if mama ain't happy because her attitude affects everyone around her.

The trouble with being happy is that it's dang hard to do. My college pastor always said "happiness

3

is a choice." I both agreed with him and gave him the stink eye. Have you ever tried to just be happy for any length of time? It works well enough until the kids start fighting, the pipes start leaking, or your jeans won't fit because you've still got the post-pregnancy love handles.

Nowadays, many moms are not only unhappy, we're anxious and depressed at unprecedented levels.[1] We are weary, worn out, and over life by 9:30 every morning. Even the smallest thing, like spilled yogurt on the counter, can send us into an absolute tizzy that scares the kids and makes us feel guilty for days.

Surprisingly, convenience hasn't made us any happier. We can set our coffee makers and washing machines on timers to fit our schedule. Groceries, household necessities, and clothes are delivered to our doorstep in a day or two. I even get air filters delivered automatically every three months to ensure I'm keeping pollutants and allergens out of our home's air. Online banking and telehealth doctor visits . . . it's all there. At our fingertips.

What a life!

Even with all that, do we feel more relaxed? More at peace? More content? Are we smelling more roses? The answer is no—somehow we are not. The smell of roses is not as strong as the odor from our baby's dirty diaper, the laundry that needs washing, and the organic produce in the refrigerator going bad.

Instead of using automation to enjoy life more, we just cross those things off our master list before adding a few more to-do items to make sure we're doing everything possible to be more efficient, organized, and productive. If we don't, we're lazy, aren't we?

That was my mindset the day of the winter field trip. Do something educational with the kids, check. Take social media–worthy photos, check. Be an exciting homeschool mom, check. I was not prepared for how quickly life could be turned upside down.

THE END OF THE WORLD AS I KNEW IT

While changing clothes after church a few days following our field trip to the botanical gardens, I noticed something odd on my left breast. I hoped it was a friction rub from all the jumping but called the doctor first thing the next morning. I went in for tests, and about a month later I was diagnosed with an early staged aggressive form of invasive breast cancer.

At the time, I thought it was the worst thing that had ever happened to me. Remarkably, in spite of all the pain and grief that followed, that scary Sunday was the beginning of the best year of my life. Certainly not easy, but still the best.

As soon as I was diagnosed, life as I knew it changed. Things that once seemed important felt pointless. Ways I used to spend my time seemed stupid. Worries and anxieties about the future were just too much. I could no longer orient my days toward a future I wasn't sure I would have.

Intuitively knowing it would make me feel better, I stopped scrolling social media. Everyone's fake tans and new shoes and clean houses seemed so superficial when I was busy sobbing on the floor of my two-year-old's bedroom, wondering whether, if I died, he'd remember me.

My husband came in once when I was in my youngest child's room crying. He had gotten used to this sight since I'd been diagnosed and asked gently, "What are you thinking about?"

Between ugly cries, I said, "I don't think I have any memories of when I was two or three years old." He didn't have an answer.

In fact, my choice to homeschool was largely driven by my desire to show the kids how much I cherished them, day in and day out. My own parents had divorced when I was young, and my dad was never around. As a child, I'd personally created a rule for the universe that said "kids shouldn't lose their parents," so the idea that my youngest child might not remember me was too much to bear.

My husband looked at me with both compassion and sadness and let me cry. I cried so often. "I have spent years with the kids, loving them all day every day. . . but they're so young," I said with a hiccup. "Maybe that love will set them up for a good life even if they don't remember me."

I was learning something important: When you are faced with a crisis, your priorities immediately become clear. All the "extra" activities have to stop, and the first to go are usually those things you've wanted to stop doing for a long time. The things you did out of guilt: Extracurriculars that drain family life with little positive upside. Weekly lessons your child fights tooth and nail. Or outside commitments you keep up, even though your heart isn't in them and you know others could do better than you.

Once those are gone, you're left with the basics. During my treatment, I couldn't even do those. I'd gone from home-schooling five kids and running a big online business to lying on my California king–sized bed all day, a big, sobbing mess who prayed she'd live. My mom, a retired schoolteacher, did schoolwork with the kids. Which was lucky for them, I suppose. My mother-in-law flew over from Australia. She helped with the kids and did all the dishes and my laundry. The kids started doing more chores. My husband took on more daily household tasks. Families from church and friends brought meals over.

I was forced, by my own physical limits, to stop nearly everything I'd filled my days with before. I took naps when I was tired. I wrote in my journal when my head was full. I texted and called friends who offered encouraging words of life. I read the Bible nearly nonstop, trying to encourage myself and find purpose in the pain.

A funny thing started to happen while I was worried I was dying. I started desiring to live. Not to survive, but to actually enjoy my life instead of just checking things off my to-do list.

I remember going for a walk and noticing the leaves on the trees. I would stop and stare at flowers and think, *These are the loveliest flowers I've ever seen.* Our gorgeous Florida sunsets would bring tears to my eyes. Even listening to the

> I think happiness may be a natural by-product of wise living.

kids arguing seemed precious and special. So much I had taken for granted before cancer (henceforth BC) suddenly seemed important. Lovely. Worth taking time for.

Nowadays, I'm not so certain happiness is a choice. Sure, I can choose to look at the bright side, focus on the positive, and write in my gratitude journal, but if my life is organized in a way that makes me unhappy, it's a constant uphill battle. I think happiness may be a natural by-product of wise living. It comes when our needs are met and we're at peace with our lives.

Even with cancer, I found peace again. Maybe for the first time.

Lessons I took with me . . .

During my lowest lows, God met and changed my entire inner world. I repented. I forgave. I felt lighter and more reflective. Because I had time to think and evaluate what my life had become, I started noticing some patterns.

I started paying attention to myself too. I discovered the spiritual, emotional, physical, and mental areas of my life I'd been neglecting. I noticed where I'd ignored God-given limits and boundaries that suddenly seemed obvious to me.

During treatment, I stopped trying to do everything, started asking for help, and no longer apologized when I needed some time to myself. I acted like my life depended on that. In some ways, it did.

I could no longer afford to sacrifice the practices of peace, quiet, rest, downtime, and sleep. I started minding my own limits and realized, with surprise, that I had once thought taking care of myself was selfish. No wonder I'd never done it! It makes sense, really. A woman seeking the narrow path of a godly life wouldn't act selfishly on purpose, so I had abandoned myself in the name of my family. This was a false dichotomy, of course. BC, the idea that I could either take good care of my family or take good care of myself existed only in my head. The more I ignored my needs, put others' wants first, and hustled more, the more selfish I became. The more I ignored myself, the more neurotic, irritable, and resentful I was. And who suffered the brunt of my ill moods?

The people who lived with me, of course.

Refusing to take care of my own physical, spiritual, mental, and emotional needs had made me anxious and strung out. Cancer taught me many things, and this question is one that came up time and time again: *Could it be that taking care of myself is not actually selfish, but maybe, just maybe, responsible?*

. . . *after making myself crazy*

In the early months of treatment, I'd been warned of something called chemo brain, which I'd been told is similar to pregnancy brain. In fact, I felt foggier and less sharp and found it harder to focus. One morning I woke to some weird feelings of déjà vu.

Déjà vu, of course, is the uncanny sensation you get when you feel you've experienced something before, even though you know you haven't. It can feel positive or negative, depending on the sensation you're "remembering." This particular morning, all my fear and anxiety came to a head, and I started having horrible sensations of déjà vu. Like something terrible had happened and was happening again.

At first this feeling emerged every ten or fifteen minutes, which was already abnormal. Then it started happening every few minutes. Then multiple times per minute. Over and over I had horrible rolling sensations of déjà vu. If that wasn't enough, my upper arm began hurting. Even though breast cancer doesn't really "go to the arm" and there'd been no evidence of metastasis, I became hysterical, convinced that the cancer had spread to my brain and to my arm.

I knew worrying wouldn't add an hour to my life,[2] but I felt powerless to overcome it.

While my mom was reading to the kids to give me some space, I walked to our backyard and called my patient advocate, a two-time breast cancer survivor. I described my feelings of dread and the stabs of pain in my arm. My voice was shaking, and I paced back and forth on the railroad ties in our yard, terrified of what my symptoms could mean.

"I think I have chemo brain or maybe worse, I don't know. I can't think straight, and I am having constant déjà vu. Maybe I'm losing my mind. My arm hurts, and it's making me panic. What should I do?"

In her kind and gentle voice she said, "These feelings are normal. It's okay. Aches and pains can come with treatment, and this doesn't sound like chemo or even cancer. It might be the worry that's causing it all."

In fact, after our phone call, my déjà vu and arm pain went away. Turns out my déjà vu was panic induced, and my arm hurt because my neck and shoulders were tense. From worry. I had been so anxious I had given myself déjà vu, which made me so stressed that I tensed my neck, which made my arm hurt. You can't make this stuff up.

After that humbling episode, I knew something had to be done about my fear and worry. The Bible tells us not to worry or be afraid more than 360 times. Sure, it's normal to worry when you are faced with a bad diagnosis. But I'd been stressed, worried, and anxious my whole life. And a fat lot of good it had done me.

I'd ended up with cancer.

I knew, going forward, for however many years I had left, I could no longer live a life I wanted to escape. If my own daily life seemed too much to bear, something had to give. I was going to believe the promises of God's Word. I was going to pay attention to my mental, physical, emotional, and spiritual boundaries.

My life depended on it.

WHAT MY PURPLE CHEVY TAUGHT ME ABOUT LIVING WISELY

For years I'd read about boundaries. And, honestly, I always thought boundaries were rules you put in place for other people because you thought they needed to change. Like the decision not to talk to toxic relatives so they'd get the hint

IF MAMA AIN'T HAPPY

and "act right." Or not to answer phone calls from friends who drained you with all their (easily solvable if they followed your advice) problems. Or to give an addicted spouse an ultimatum to prevent relapse.

Turns out, those are rules. But they aren't boundaries.

Boundaries aren't arbitrary behaviors we decide that we (or others) should or should not do. This is why you can't just adopt someone else's boundaries like a formula. Why not? Because they are personal and person-specific.

Boundaries are, in essence, our limits. They are the lines that, when crossed, result in dis-ease and disease.

You don't really decide your own boundaries; they simply are. If you don't function on less than eight hours of sleep, you can't pencil five hours into your planner and think you'll be okay. You can't decide what your physical limits are; you simply have to respect them.

This is where we've gotten ourselves mixed up. We may decide we're going to get up super early, do a HIIT workout, read our Bibles, meal plan for the day, tidy the house, make a hot breakfast for the kids, do organized activities with them all morning, work during naptime, put the kids to bed by seven, then stay up until midnight with our spouse for some quality time. Just because we make such a plan doesn't mean it is a pace we can maintain.

We can decide how far we want to push ourselves, but that doesn't change when we'll give out. That's a lesson my first car taught me.

When I turned sixteen, my mom bought me a Chevy

12

Cavalier that was the color of purple orchids. Try getting into trouble in a small town with a purple car. Best of luck.

Well, I loved that car, and to make it more personal, I put a photo of my friends and me on the dashboard. Then one day when I cranked it in the high school parking lot after volleyball practice, smoke began billowing out of the hood. A lot of smoke.

As it turns out, I had cracked my engine block. Because I hadn't changed my oil. Because I hadn't seen the "change oil" light come on. Because I had a photo over the dashboard lights.

What an expensive lesson that was.

There came a point when my car couldn't go on as it was. I didn't decide when that should be; it was the moment it couldn't carry on any longer in its condition.

And that's how we are. We can push ourselves however hard, fast, or far we want. But if we don't mind our own boundaries, we may break down before we get where we're trying to go.

Sounds simple, right? Just figure out your own limits and then stick to them. The problem is, the world sends us a lot of messages about what makes a good mom, a nurturing home, and a successful life. And then those cues are reinforced by social media or even well-meaning friends. Many of these messages are, at best, unhelpful and, at worst, destructive.

Recognizing, and debunking, some of these messages will prepare you to start moving toward a happier and healthier family life—so that's where our journey will begin. Until you and I begin to name and reject some of these unhealthy messages, all the external voices are likely to drown out the still, quiet one inside of you.

CHAPTER 2

Sending the Wrong Message

I CAN STILL PICTURE MYSELF several years ago, lying on the couch taking a break while my toddler and preschooler napped. We were living in Australia at the time. I was pregnant with our third child and had spent all day with our little ones in our small townhome while my husband was at school. Did I nap? Read a good book? Do a handiwork project? No, it was too easy to pick up my phone and start scrolling through seemingly endless social media photos showing smiling families traveling the world. They always seemed to be swimming with dolphins or taking African safaris. The message I got was: *Don't have a boring life!* As someone who loved to travel but was currently strapped for cash and caring for our growing family, that message caused a lot of discontent. Did I stop scrolling? No, I kept scrolling, and the more photos I saw, the less satisfied with my own life I became.

A few years later, I came across an admonition from Hillary Morgan Ferrer in the book *Mama Bear Apologetics* to "Recognize the message."[1] She says the first step to resisting the cultural lies around us is to really pay attention to what we hear or see each day. I believe this is foundational if we want to recognize and live within our limits as mothers and women. We need to actively keep the good and throw out the bad messages we're given. In fact, many of us will discover that we need to set limits around some areas in our lives (the news, for example) simply because receiving all that information without discrimination or discernment will take us from being happy to terrified in a heartbeat.

That is no way to live.

So what are some common messages that can actually push us into anxiety, stress, overwhelm, and unhappiness? No doubt there are more than I have listed here, but I've chosen these particular messages because they seem to make a big difference in whether a mother is happy or not. And her contentment makes a huge difference in the entire family's well-being.

These messages seem to leak out into many areas of our lives and can do a lot of damage. Luckily, once we recognize them, we can begin to counteract them and make real changes that lead to freedom.

Message #1: If our children aren't happy, we are bad parents.

Of course we don't set out to make our children unhappy. We love them more than life itself and never want them to feel unnecessarily rejected, upset, or down. Yet when we imagine it's possible to parent in a way that will always make our children happy, we begin an elusive quest—all day, every day—to avoid causing them any displeasure or discomfort.

The problem comes when we avoid enforcing beneficial boundaries that ensure our kids get enough sleep, proper food, and limits around their behavior because we don't want them to be unhappy. In recent years this message has exploded on the scene. It manifests in three main ways.

One, if a rule, routine, or request we make to our children results in their unhappiness, tears, or meltdowns, then it was not a good idea in the first place. If we make our children do things that cause distress, it means we're trying to control them, which is bad.

Scene: Child throws a fit in the mornings before school because he'd rather stay home with Mom.

Mom: Can't figure out the reason for her child's resistance. Has ruled out bullying, learning disorders, and other obvious reasons a child might refuse to go to school. Even so, decides it is wrong to make the child go to school when he is so distressed, so she lets the child stay home a lot of the time.

Child: Perfectly happy at home.

Mom: *It's better for him to be happy at home than for me to force him to do something he obviously hates.*

Two, if our children are frustrated and upset by our rules and we force them to follow them anyway, we may damage their physical, mental, or emotional health.

Scene: Mom is nearly finished cooking dinner when a little one comes up, asking for a snack.

Mom: "Dinner's almost ready. Then you can eat."

Child: Weeping and gnashing of teeth.

Mom: Thinks, *Surely she can wait, but . . . maybe she is really hungry . . . she's going to feel like I'm starving her . . . maybe it's actually wrong of me to deprive her of something I have . . . what's a little snack?* She hands her daughter a granola bar.

Dinner: Child barely eats.

Mom: Feels resentful.

Three, if our children are upset or unhappy with our rule, routine, or request and we follow through with it anyway, we are not being emotionally responsive. What good mother wants to feel like she is abandoning her children emotionally? None. So we feel guilty, stressed, and anxious because we can't handle any of their overwhelming emotions. If we were "good moms," our kids would always be happy.

Scene: Daughter asks for a smartphone because all her friends have one.

Mom: Feels it's too early and unnecessary at this life stage.

Child: Whines that she'll be left out from friend group; creates lots of power battles; says Mom is ruining her life; sheds lots of tears.

Mom: Second-guesses choice; feels darned if she does, darned if she doesn't; gives in despite her intuition; quickly regrets her choice.

If we believe this message that we are only good mothers when our children are happy, then we cannot enforce healthy meals, appropriate bedtimes, reasonable self-care, hygiene routines, or anything that goes against our children's moods. We cannot require them to go to school, the dentist, or the grocery store with us because they don't feel like it.

Once we internalize this message, we begin to develop a lot of shady tricks to try to make our kids happy with our rules. We bribe, cajole, and twist their arms instead of lovingly and firmly holding our family boundaries, knowing they are for everyone's ultimate good.

Our brains say, *I want to enforce this,* but our emotions tell us, *Do whatever it takes to make this child stop crying!* We are so triggered by our children's emotions that we cannot think straight. Instead of believing that emotions are a part of life and allowing our children to learn to process them even as we keep reasonable boundaries, we abandon what's good for them long-term to stop them from crying in the short-term. This leads to insecure mothers at the mercy of our children's moods rather than secure, nurturing parents who act out of love.

This message also carries over into a similar and related one: *that we should make life as easy as possible for our kids.* If we believe this, that means when things get hard and the kids get upset, we jump into rescuer mode. We swoop in with our superhero mom capes to rescue our kids from a hard life. This doesn't make their lives easier, either. In fact, it makes life harder when they grow into adults because they realize they no longer have anyone to rescue them.

If you have taken in this message, dear mom, it's very difficult to make choices for your children. Because if your decision makes them unhappy, you were wrong. If it frustrates them, you were wrong. Even if you know you are setting a healthy limit backed by research (like limited screen time), you will toss to and fro with your child's emotions if you believe all your choices should make the kids happy.

When a generation of moms get in the habit of giving their kids all the privileges and ease that actually come in adulthood (lots of screen time, staying up late, choice over all aspects of life) without any of the responsibilities, we end up with a generation of kids who don't want to grow up.

Message #2: We must give our kids every opportunity we can.

When they're little, this probably looks like toys and activities. We so desire to give our children the best that we spend money we don't have and time we can never get back driving them to sports, lessons, or activities they may not even like. We buy endless toys that they play with once and then discard. Talk about commitment on our part!

I had a colleague who would end up in knock-down, drag-out fights with her preschooler in the parking lot of the dance studio. I often wondered why she put herself and her daughter through such a scene for ballet lessons the little girl didn't even like. For the photos?

The idea that we should give our children every possible opportunity comes from a desire to set our kids up for lifelong success and happiness. Naturally, loving mothers want their children to have good lives. If we can offer them these good experiences while they are under our roofs, then by Jove we will do so.

Another reason many mothers bend over backwards and spin themselves in circles to give their children every opportunity is that their own parents didn't offer them this support when they were children. These parents will often make it a subconscious goal to give their children the very thing they themselves missed out on.

In past decades, setting children up for a good life often meant teaching them character traits like responsibility and hard work or helping youth find jobs or get into college. But to many moms today, this means doing everything we can to ensure our children are as experienced or well-rounded as possible.

In theory, this sounds lovely. In practice, this may lead to an overscheduled, chaotic, stress-inducing life. We want our kids to master an instrument, play a sport, learn another language, be on the debate team, join a LEGO club, start a YouTube channel, open an Etsy shop for their art, and anything else that might make a good impression on a college application. All before elementary school is over.

If you and your children are naturally stress-free people with low sleep needs and no tendency toward overstimulation, this approach may work well for your family. But for most families, this strategy will lead to trouble.

After all, you are the one who has to organize an overfilled schedule and cart everyone around all week to activities that may cause a lot of anxiety and time away from home. Second, kids usually don't care that much about most of the things we want them to do.

In fact, an overfilled life usually makes our children stressed and tired, with little time to relax. We're now taxi drivers with no time to cook nourishing meals at home or even rest. The pace of life is so fast that it can lead to burnout. For us and the kids.

Here is the groundbreaking, hard-won, Einstein-level secret (backed by research) nobody's telling us: The best way to set up our kids for future life success is to love them enough to hold our ground and make them do their chores.

Message #3: Being anxious all the time is normal.

Anyone who has suffered from anxiety knows it is extremely disruptive. Instead of carrying on with life happily, you end up obsessing over how to avoid the unpleasant feelings you are experiencing. It can grow and take over your life.

Anxiety used to be something people were ashamed about. They would quietly suffer without knowing who to reach out to for help. Now people share about their anxiety openly, rightly wanting to remove the stigma of mental health issues. Because of this, we are seeing a massive increase in the number of women who acknowledge their struggle with depression and anxiety.

Of course, hormones—from pregnancy and nursing, sometimes over and over—play a part. Major life changes also contribute to a sense of upheaval, which makes us more anxious. Trauma, from adverse events in both childhood and adulthood, predisposes us to feeling anxious. Our nervous system seems to have a mind of its own.

During my third pregnancy, I became extremely anxious and visited a counselor. She told me something that immediately comforted me, although it didn't "fix" anything: "It makes perfect sense that you're anxious. In the past five years, you've gotten married, gotten pregnant, had babies, moved homes, and emigrated overseas. All of these are in the top ten life stressors for women." Well, no wonder. When I moved into my second trimester, that particular spell with anxiety vanished. Although it turned out to be hormonal, I hung on to my counselor's words.

There is now a widespread cultural discussion normalizing anxiety. On the one hand, this is desperately needed. It is encouraging and validating to women who are suffering.

On the other hand, discussions around anxiety often imply that there's nothing we can do about it. Which just isn't true.

Some personalities, life experiences, and hormonal imbalances make women more susceptible to anxiety. That's not debatable. In fact, because so many women are prone to anxiety due to factors outside of their control, it's critical that we organize our family life in a way that promotes peace.

My Christian friends often berate themselves for their anxiety, intuitively feeling they should not be living in a state of worry, yet not knowing how to get out of it. Often that's because we think we should be able to live frantic, overfilled, overscheduled lives without anxiety, instead of recognizing that by simplifying our lives, we would have fewer reasons to be anxious in the first place.

Anxieties related strictly to chemical imbalances and hormones aside, the real problem is that we can't turn a blind eye to many of the people and activities that cause us stress—like our children and our chores. Many areas of our lives can seem out of control, and making meaningful, permanent changes sometimes feels like too much.

Often we wait to address this problem until we are so anxious that we feel paralyzed and as if we're on the brink of a nervous breakdown. Yet there are a number of proven ways to get unstuck and eliminate stress and anxiety. Try them if you dare.

Practice prayer and meditation. Choose verses from Scripture that speak into your current life phase, write them in your journal, save them on your phone, revisit them when you are feeling discouraged or down, and then lean on those promises like your life depends on it. I have some go-to verses that always help me recenter my mind and heart.

Get off your devices. This is tough for all of us without accountability. Add time-tracking apps or build "no phone times" into your day. Remove apps that are time suckers or that bring discontentment. Instead of walking around with your device, plug it into a charging station or keep it out of sight for large chunks of the day. I'll purposefully leave my phone out of reach to take advantage of the "out of sight, out of mind" principle. Plus, this helps me see that sometimes checking my phone feels urgent, but if I wait five minutes, I realize I don't even remember why I wanted to check it in the first place.

Quit a job you don't like. Scary, but worth considering. Even the realization that you don't have to stay at a job you hate forever may bring some relief. Begin praying about a possible job move, research other companies in your field that may have job openings, and start embracing the possibilities a new job might bring you.

Sell a car or house that costs too much money and weighs you down with debt. This is another idea that may feel very scary at first, but then you may wonder why it took so long to do afterward. Find out what your car or home is worth, determine whether it's feasible to sell and downsize, then start imagining what it would feel like to have that extra money in your account each month.

Live within your means. Get help from friends or experts to lower your budget. Spending can be fun but often results in an unpleasant hangover. Determine whether you have an "income problem" or a "spending problem," and make changes accordingly. There is a lot of satisfaction in knowing you have even a little bit of money left over at the end of the month.

Discard all the junk, clutter, and mess in your home. This can be a weekend project or a more gradual one. Removing clutter will immediately lift your mood, so it may be easier than you expect, even if you tend toward hoarding. Less stuff means less to clean, less to organize, and less to think about. Fewer clothes equals less laundry. Fewer toys equals quicker cleanup. You get the idea.

Forgive those who have hurt you. Forgiveness is immensely difficult and equally healing. Once you grieve your pain and hurt, you can decide it's time to put the past behind you. Realize that forgiveness is not so much an act of mercy for the other person as it is a gift to yourself.

Set boundaries with people who take advantage of you. Often we don't even realize that our own lack of boundaries makes it possible for people to overstep without any hurdles. Start small and set boundaries to protect your own sanity. (See chapter 3 for a definition of boundaries and ideas on how to begin setting them.)

Drop extracurriculars that take too much time. Nothing is forever; if you need a break from the chauffeur life for a while, you can take one. Choose activities that are closer to home, organize lessons on specific days, or take certain semesters off to add some breathing room.

Exercise to release endorphins and regulate hormones.
Don't neglect visiting your doctor about any health concerns
related to anxiety, but know that moving your body is proven to
help with anxiety over time. Walks are sufficient and, in fact,
often better than more extreme exercise, which can elevate
stress levels.

Eat well. Instead of going on a restrictive diet that causes you
anxiety when you even think about it, just focus on adding more
fruit and vegetables to your meals. Noticing how your body
feels after eating certain foods will help you choose the ones
that make you feel good.

Face your problems head-on instead of avoiding them.
Trying to escape your feelings and problems is like incurring
credit card debt. It may boost your mood in the moment, but
you will have to deal with the fallout sometime. Putting them off
just compounds the interest. There's no time like the present to
write out all the things that cause you stress and address them
one by one.

Get enough rest. Sleep is survival. Without enough sleep, our
brains begin to struggle to carry out even the most basic of
functions. We get brain fog and impaired judgment, and small
things suddenly become huge when we are perpetually
exhausted.

**Choose not to live in fear of the future or "what ifs";
instead, trust in God.** This may sound unrealistic, but as we
really work to make our thought life reflect our faith, it gets
easier and easier. Those of us prone to anxiety and worry may
still see it rear its ugly head from time to time, but we absolutely
can organize our lives so they are more peaceful and happy.

Anyone telling you otherwise wants to sell you their solution. Which leads me to the next damaging message mothers regularly receive.

Message #4: Life will be better when . . .

Since our culture is so oriented toward the future, we attach our happiness to attaining those goals we are slaving toward. We'll be happy when our home is bigger. When our baby sleeps through the night. When we pay off our student loans. When the kids are in school. When we get that lake house. When our business gets off the ground.

> Do not boast about tomorrow, for you do not know what a day may bring.
>
> Proverbs 27:1, NIV

To make it more personal: I would be more happy if I lost fifteen pounds. If the kids would stop fighting. If my husband helped out around the house more. If the kitchen was renovated. If I had a fancier car.

And on and on and on.

I bet goal-setting is a billion-dollar business. There are books, workbooks, courses, systems, and expensive masterminds who will teach you how to set outlandish goals that scare you, then help you break it all down into bite-sized tasks that you need to do every day.

If the goal doesn't scare you, it's not big enough!

True, if we want to get somewhere in our future, we must start purposefully moving in that direction. We can't expect to get our groceries for the week without either driving to the grocery store or ordering them online.

What's also true is that a fixation on the future sacrifices our present. And even more sobering, we only have the present and are guaranteed no future.

What happens when we put off our current happiness to some point in the future, when some Specific Thing happens? We become unhappy today. Instead of enjoying the blessings we have now—our children at their current ages, our home (even if it's too small), our bodies that wake up each day—we are discontented.

We have given outside circumstances control over our moods. And thus over our lives. Instead of learning to appreciate what is today and still work toward what we want for our family's future, we become future-obsessed as we sacrifice the now.

When I was diagnosed with cancer and faced the prospect of dying young, I came face-to-face with the reality that I was too focused on the future. I plotted, schemed, and saved with such anxiety, desperate to better our family's situation. In reality our family's situation was fine; my own heart was not. I wanted more, bigger, better "for the kids," and many times, in the process, I forgot to enjoy my kids. How many precious moments had passed me by while I was mentally distracted, worried about some trivial thing or another? How many days had I complained about the home I was living in, instead of thanking God for shelter and then getting on the floor to play with the kids?

When going through chemo, feeling sick and tired, I'd sit outside in our unfinished wild country backyard and think, *What a beautiful place we live in.* I'd watch the kids, look into their faces, hear their laughter, and wonder what I had been so obsessed with before. How could I orient my life around a future that was not guaranteed?

> But godliness with contentment is great gain. For we brought nothing into the world, and we can take nothing out of it.
>
> 1 Timothy 6:6-7, NIV

My stress and anxiety about the future, as well as my desire for more and more, had cost me.

Sure, plan and be wise for the future. Be a good steward of your resources. Make prudent steps in the direction you want to go. But not at the expense of the present. Not from a place of obsession or fear.

Life will not improve if you continually live in a cycle of looking to a future that isn't guaranteed. In fact, this mindset only makes you unhappy and resentful in the present. That leads to the final message that is making mothers unhappy today.

Message #5: We are in full control of our lives.

It's partly true that we are in control. We are in control of our daily choices and actions. We decide what we say to those around us. We choose what we want to cook or where we want to go on vacation.

We also choose our spouses. Our clothes and home decor

reflect our own styles. We decide how much money we will spend or save. There are many areas in our lives in which we are in control from day to day. And, of course, we know that our daily decisions and choices affect our futures.

We want to believe that happiness is outside of our control and that it will fall upon us like a pancake from heaven if the circumstances are just right. No Christian woman would actually agree that joy comes from our circumstances, but without realizing it, we think and live as if this were true. We put responsibility for our happiness on a bunch of factors that may or may not happen. Many of which are outside of our control.

And yet at the same time . . . we are not in control. We can save faithfully and lose our money in a stock market crash one month before retirement. We can work diligently for a company and lose our job. Spouses can be unfaithful, teenagers can make self-destructive choices, and tragedies can happen.

Now that you are encouraged, I want to highlight why it matters that we know we are not ultimately in control. Because when we feel in complete control, we begin to obsess about every choice and action. We think the weight of the entire world is on our shoulders, and every choice takes on life-or-death importance. We think that if we do everything right and are Very Good Moms, then nothing bad will happen to our families.

If we hear of a tragedy happening to someone else, we dissect that person's choices. We want to figure out what they did wrong so we do *not* do that and avoid their fate.

We begin to take on more and more responsibility so we can feel in control of even more and prevent anything bad from happening to us or those we love.

Rather than fool proofing and safeguarding our lives, however, that strategy crushes us. As God told Job, we did not hang the moon and the stars in the sky or set the seas in place; nor do we control the rain or snow (see Job 38). We intuitively know we are not in control, but we live in such fear of what's to come that we try to control everything to prevent disaster.

It is a recipe for anxiety, distress, and unhappiness.

The way forward is not easy, but it is simple. We do our best to care for our families, but we accept that we cannot guarantee a trouble-free future for them. Trying to control more and more in an attempt to prevent anything bad from happening will not actually stop bad things; it will bring bad things upon us.

Like overwhelm, exhaustion, depression, burnout, and anxiety.

The solution is to place our trust in the God of the universe who can bring good out of any situation (Romans 8:28); to accept that fear and anxiety sometimes come without warning, but that we can decide whether we want to remain rooted in them; and to choose to believe we will be okay, no matter what.

The day before I got my cancer diagnosis, I stood during church and asked for prayer. A six-time cancer-surviving friend of mine walked with me outside after the service to offer some encouragement. Tall, calm, beautiful, and full of assurance, she said to me, "Rachel, it's going to be okay."

I looked at her like she had antlers growing out of her head. I was thinking, *Of course it's not going to be okay; I probably have cancer.* She remained unruffled and simply said, "No matter what, it will be okay."

It wasn't until I wrestled with my fear of death and came out the other side—still with cancer—that I realized she was right. No matter what happens, it will be okay. Trusting an Almighty God with whatever happens, knowing that He will never leave you nor forsake you (Deuteronomy 31:6) is the only way to sustainable peace in a world where there are threats on every corner.

Even amidst difficult circumstances, it can be okay. Even when facing unimaginable situations, we can know peace. It's true that a lot of things may go wrong in our lives. We get sideswiped, sidelined, and sidetracked by all kinds of things.

But as we've also acknowledged, you can make decisions that will lead to more peace and harmony in your home. Some of them are recognizing and rejecting the pie-in-the-sky idea that good parenting leads to kids who are always happy, that anxiety is inevitable and there's nothing you can do about it, and that the future matters more than the present. The rest of this book centers on ways to come to terms with your own limits and preferences and then structure your life around those. Doing so will lead to wisdom and, dare I say it, happiness. Are you ready?

CHAPTER 3

Hard Stop: Limits, Boundaries, and Preferences

My kids learned to ride bikes very late. We live in the country and don't even have a paved driveway, much less sidewalks nearby. They attempted to ride off and on over the years, but I was rarely inspired to load five bikes in the truck, drive twenty minutes to the nearest park, and then chase after them all while they practiced riding.

Then one spring break on Saint George Island in the Florida Panhandle, I decided enough was enough. We had three elementary-aged kids and I determined that they should know the joy of riding bikes, and I was going to make it happen. I rented some bikes, and we went out for a spin. Two of my kids picked it up instantly and were soon biking all around the back roads, experiencing the fun of feeling the wind in their faces.

Because sunsets are so lovely in Florida, we decided to chase the stunning colors that evening. The sun sets on the bay side, not the beach side, so we couldn't just plop down on the sand and behold the majesty. We needed to ride around on the back roads of the bay side of the island, looking for the perfect place to see the sun go down.

Boy, did we find a place. Between a few houses there was a little public cove piled with big rocks and a small beach area with a perfect view of the horizon. We enjoyed it so much that we began riding the bikes from our rental house to that cove each evening.

One particularly windy evening, we set off to ride toward the cove. Two of the kids were riding independently, my husband was helping another son get the hang of it, and I was riding along behind. I felt the wind whip through my curly red, salty beach hair, which is wild on a normal day, and my pretty sundress was blowing in the breeze. A very cinematic moment.

As I turned left onto the back road that would take me to the little cove, everything changed. Now I was riding straight into strong winds. Pedaling suddenly took a lot more strength, and my legs were getting shaky.

I slowed down because it required much more strength to keep moving forward. The grit from the old gravel road started flying in my eyes, making me squint and my eyes water. I had to keep my face down to keep the dust out of my eyes.

Strong gusts were blowing right toward me, my sundress started flying up over my face, and I flashed a perfectly innocent retired couple walking their thousand-dollar dog. From then on, I tried to steer the bike with one shaky hand while using the other either to hold down my dress or to keep my favorite headband from flying off my head. Priorities.

It didn't occur to me to stop and regroup, obviously, because I had somewhere to be and something to see. If I start going somewhere, I'm going to get there, even if it begins to look like a bad idea. I'm no quitter!

Exhausted and shaky, I arrived at the little cove disheveled and pretty satisfied with myself. *What's a little resistance? Take that, wind. You won't steal the sunset from me.* We enjoyed the view for a bit and then decided to head back home.

Hopping back on my bike, I turned around and headed back down that same road. And that's when the miracle happened. The same wind that had slowed me down, dirtied my face, caused me to flash the neighbors, and nearly stole my headband was now at my back. Pushing me forward. It was such a strong wind that I could coast for long stretches of time.

Grit no longer flew into my face, my outfit stayed in place, my muscles were relaxed, and I barely had to exert any effort to get where I was going. The tailwind was so strong that I was going at least twice as fast as I had on the way there when I was furiously pedaling against the wind. Now I was laughing as I was riding.

It was such a startling difference that I thought about it

for hours afterward. Because I realized that this is exactly what life can be like. When our lives seem to be in conflict with our needs, personalities, personal preferences, values, and convictions, it's as if we are riding into the wind. Everything is harder, more chaotic, less fun, and extremely draining. It's such a pain that we want to give up, and if we do arrive at our destination, we're so beaten down that we barely remember why we wanted to get there in the first place.

When our lives are organized and lived in alignment with healthy boundaries, according to our values, needs, limits, and personalities, everything is easier. It's less work. It feels more freeing and fun. Who wants to get up each morning and push into the wind all day? If from sunup to sundown, every task feels draining and every activity feels twice as hard and half as fun as it should be, take heart. You are not alone.

Later, as I contemplated my rough ride to the cove to watch the sunset, I realized I could have gotten there from a few other paths, any of which would have allowed me to avoid riding straight into the wind. We don't have to white-knuckle our way through life. There is an easier and more pleasant way.

My hope in writing this book is to remind you of the limits you know but may have forgotten since becoming a mother. And to impart wisdom for peaceful living so you aren't always fighting the wind in your face as you try to get where you're going.

THE IMMOVABLE BOUNDARIES WE CAN'T BLOW PAST

Certain things in life are obvious and indisputable. We don't try to argue with these principles because we know it's pointless. These tangible boundaries, so to speak, are walls. Years ago, a friend introduced me to the Language of Listening® coaching program for parents.[1] I've always appreciated its approach to mothering, and I like the way its founder, Sandy Blackard, defines boundaries by pointing out the obvious difference between a wall and a door.

If you are in the bedroom and want to get to the kitchen, you take the path available to get there. You head out the door. You could, of course, try throwing yourself against the wall over and over again to knock it down and let you through. But that would take a lot of energy, you'd end up injured, and you'd probably still not have a clear path to your destination.

Instead, you take the logical path—the doorway. The wall is a firm boundary.

In life, we are confronted with many firm boundaries that we simply don't fight. We acknowledge they're there and then work around them. We don't pretend they don't exist and do our own thing. Rather, we respect them.

I still remember the time I ran out of gas three blocks from the kids' school because I was trying to get to the cheapest gas station. Gas is less expensive just over the border in Alabama, so I planned to drive a few miles farther before filling up because—doggone it—I won't be bamboozled and wanted to save those three dollars. As a result, I had to walk with the kids along the busy road in a ditch until a friend pulled over and gave us a ride—all because my van quit. It was done. It simply ran out of gas and completely didn't care about my goal or my plan. I could not convince it to keep going.

Money is another example. We recognize that having one hundred dollars means we can spend up to one hundred dollars. After that, we have no more money. We may borrow, charge it, or come up with some other way to get what we want, but we are responsible for the amount of money we spend. We don't think, *You know what? I'll just spend $15,000 today on shoes, and it won't matter.* We recognize that our finances are limited, and we aim to spend only what we have. In fact, if we end up spending more than we have, not only do we owe what we spent, but the interest on our purchase means we're in debt for even more. A penalty, if you will, on having overspent in the first place.

We recognize that if we stop paying our mortgage, we'll eventually lose the house. If we stop paying our rent, we'll eventually be evicted. If we don't pay the electric bill, the lights will go off. Stop paying the car payment, and it will be repossessed. These boundaries are not something we can push through; they are something we work to live within.

As a beach lover, I recognize the shoreline as a boundary. At one point I am on sand, but if I

> Tangible boundaries are walls; they are something we work to live within.

keep walking toward the water, my feet will get wet. Next I'll be submerged in the waves, and eventually I won't be able to touch the bottom. I understand this will happen and don't go out farther than is safe. Similarly, if you take your boat too close to shore, you will run aground. No one keeps steering the boat closer to shore while the motor is churning up sand. We respect the obvious physical boundary.

INVISIBLE BOUNDARIES? WE IGNORE THEM

You probably shook your head as you were reading the examples above, thinking how obvious they are. What is less obvious, however, are the invisible boundaries. Many of the less obvious, intangible boundaries and limits exist within us, but we tend to ignore them because the consequences aren't instant or may even seem unrelated.

Take sleep, for example. We've all heard the average adult needs seven to eight hours of sleep per night for optimal health and performance. We believe this to be true, but we also know we can get less sleep than that for days on end without dying.

Sure, we may get so tired that we need coffee all day to stay awake and then need to take melatonin, Ambien, or a glass of wine to fall asleep at night, but hey, we can survive with less sleep. Try us.

The boundary line doesn't seem that obvious. It's definitely not firm in our minds because we seem to be doing okay even if we sleep less. But research is clear, concise, and irrefutable: Lack of sleep causes anxiety, depression, memory loss, a decrease in the ability to regulate behavior and moods, decreased immune response, and exponential increase in risk factors relating to both cancer and other metabolic diseases. Plus, there is no denying that we are just plain in a crabby mood when we're tired.

Every mother on earth has limited time, emotional energy, physical energy, brain space, bandwidth, and abilities. The key to living a peaceful, happy life is recognizing your own limits and respecting them. Instead of drinking caffeine to stay awake and popping pills to get to sleep, you could simply prioritize sleep. If you can't sleep because your children won't sleep, you really *can* teach your children to sleep.

If you need help teaching healthy sleep habits to your little ones, learn my sustainable sleep solutions at *learn.sleeplittlelamb.com.*

Whether we ignore them or not, certain limits are always there. The effects of sleep deprivation come out sideways in our mood and health, but they don't seem quite as severe or firm as getting kicked out of our house for not paying the mortgage. The cost of ignoring these natural limits may seem so subtle that we don't notice it, but it is insidious all the same.

We mothers are experts at applying Band-Aids. We are so good at getting to the end of our rope, tying a knot, and hanging on for dear life. For years at a time. We can ride into a proverbial headwind, go to bed aching, and wake up the next day to do it again. We are bullheaded and relentless.

We have developed perseverance, grit, and diligence. We give generously and sacrificially to our families. We would do anything for them and, in fact, would put their needs, wants, and desires above our own without a second thought—even if doing so makes us mentally, physically, and emotionally ill. We love our kids so much that we will make ourselves sick to be sure they get everything we think they should have. No good mom will prioritize her own life above the lives of her kids. Never.

If this describes you, I feel both your weariness and resolve. The resolve to be the best mother you can be for your kids. The weariness that comes from riding into a strong wind, day in, day out, and seeing no other path to get where you want to go.

Thankfully, and because God can use all things for our good, all that wind resistance has refined you. Your muscles are stronger, and you've shown you will do whatever it takes to get where you're going. You've gotten back up when you've fallen down, and you have not given up. Your trials have produced steadfastness, and you have proven yourself a loving mother.

And now, you can find a different path to your destination.

WHY FIGURING OUT YOUR BOUNDARIES CAN BE HARD

By now we see that ignoring our limits and boundaries doesn't go well for us. But how do we figure out our limits?

How do we recognize these invisible boundaries we've been ignoring for so long?

I think it's a simple (though not easy) three-step process: We unearth them, mark them, and put up flags or fences to pinpoint their location. Let me explain.

My husband is a drafter for a surveying company. When someone wants to sell or purchase a piece of property, a survey of that property is a must. To get this document, surveyors go to the land, uncover the boundary lines, and mark them. These boundary markers are iron rods typically placed in the corners of the lot that help show where the property ends or begins.

Once the surveyors find these markers, they place pin or marking flags in the ground to point out the property lines. Often, they'll put ribbons in the trees at these lines as well. They want the lines visible to make it easier for the buyers, sellers, neighbors, or construction workers who may be coming to put up a fence or build structures on the property.

The markers that help define the boundary lines are nearly always there, but sometimes they are buried. If the surveyors can't see the markers, they will use metal detectors to find them. And this may be what you have to do to find your boundary markers.

It's time to go digging.

Our feelings are a good place to start. While our feelings can be bad masters, they are good advisors. (More on that in chapter 8.) Are we feeling bitter, resentful, angry, weary, depressed, anxious, or hopeless?

Beep, beep, beep, something is buried below.

Many moms—certainly most Christian moms—heap guilt on themselves when they feel those hidden emotions from above. I remember feeling unhappy one evening after a hard day and then immediately chiding myself because I knew so many people were far worse off than me. I told myself that it was selfish to be unhappy and that I should repent. I remember visualizing taking all my feelings and putting them into a container with a lid. Because I was living in an unsustainable way, I felt awful, and then I condemned myself for having those natural feelings. The problem was, as hard as I tried to stuff them down, they didn't go away. They just came out sideways.

Can you relate? Throw on a bit of shame for not doing everything perfectly and some fear that the whole world will implode if we don't get things right and, well, you have the modern mom. Anxious, fearful, guilty, and ticked off. But looking cute on social.

Our feelings may be so strong that we don't even know which boundary lines have been crossed and which limits have been ignored. Trying to untangle everything may feel overwhelming at first. And to some degree, it will be. Seeing all the areas of your life and realizing how far you are living from your own limits can be daunting.

Let's take the home. Your own preferences, personality, and natural temperament might mean you like things to be fairly tidy. Not perfect, but not a big mess. Say you have three kids who love making messes (don't all kids?), and no one helps you clean up afterward. You try to convince yourself you don't care and tell yourself that it'll be less messy in a few years. You might even remind yourself how much you'll miss the peanut butter handprints on the windows when the kids are gone.

This may be what you think. But it isn't what you feel. What you feel is resentment, bitterness, stress, and anger because you hate a dirty house and now you're living in one. And you're paying for it. Figuratively and literally. The environment in your own home goes against your natural inclinations; the result is a feeling of unease. You can pretend you don't care, but you do care.

You'll get mad when you see messes, and you'll probably end up yelling at the kids. *Here they go again, making a mega fort that'll take an hour to clean up.* Don't miss the message that is bubbling up inside you in that moment: You've uncovered a boundary marker. You need the home to be relatively tidy. Or at a minimum, you want to be able to get it into a tidy state without spending days doing so. And you want some help.

So . . . now what?

You've figured out a personal boundary. It's clear you've been living in an environment *you do not like* in the home *that you pay for*, and you want to make a change. What do you do?

Put a flag on it! Just as someone might put up a fence around their property line, create some routines, rhythms, or rules to protect your own boundary.

RULES AND ROUTINES HELP PROTECT YOUR BOUNDARY LINES

1. We've discovered a way we are living that keeps us stressed (e.g., a perpetually messy house).

2. We've put a pin flag in the ground (acknowledging this area matters to us, no matter what we try and pretend).

3. Now we build structures to protect that boundary, like a homeowner who puts a fence along a boundary line (e.g., creating routines or rules to keep the home tidy).

In a nutshell, that's how to create a life of peace. In the coming chapters, we will break down the biggest areas of life that tend to stress us moms. We will explore how you can discover your own boundaries or limits, put a flag in them, and then build structures around them to protect them.

You'll discover where you've been riding into the wind, working harder than you have to. Instead of adopting the current cultural ideas that try to convince us that we are not limited by anything, I want us to embrace our God-given limits so we can be at peace. Limits exist in nature, and they exist within us. You may be able to defy nature for a while, but it will always win out. As the popular old country song says, "Don't outsmart your common sense."[2]

I want to show you that you can care for yourself well, *not at the expense of your precious family*, but because doing so will help you become the woman God designed you to be. And when you are not spending your whole life riding into the wind, you'll have far more energy and joy to give to your family.

It's a win-win. Let's get started.

CHAPTER 4

Transforming Losing Situations into Win-Win Solutions

As a mom of young kids in this current social media age, I am not surprised by much. Having received thousands of emails over the years from guilt-laden, sleep-deprived mothers, I am not new to moms' internal struggles when it comes to setting limits. Many moms think our only choices are to (1) do what's best for our kids or (2) take care of ourselves and therefore damage our kids.

But even I was taken aback one day while working toward my infant and child sleep certification when a colleague shared an interaction she had on her social media platform. She was sharing some practical baby sleep strategies when a mother chimed in to insist that any form of sleep intervention was wrong. That no matter the cost, you must never put yourself before your baby.

On the surface, most of us would agree with this. We wait so patiently for our precious babies. Or maybe when we are heavily pregnant, we wait impatiently eating eggplant and pineapple and then doing what got us pregnant in the first place to get us un-pregnant as fast as possible. It's true—we want what's best for our children and almost instinctively think of our children before ourselves.

But soon this mom's story got weird. She said her baby never napped and woke up twenty-plus times a night—and had done so since birth. By around seven months postpartum, the woman was admitted to the hospital for extreme sleep deprivation and exhaustion. Now most people would agree that, after an event like this, it was time to make some changes to keep both mom and baby well. But this mother? Nope. Even though she was exhausted and malnourished to the point that she'd been on a feeding tube, she was quick to say that she continued to respond to her baby's every movement and ignore her own body completely.

She could barely stay awake during the day to watch her little one and found herself dropping off to sleep randomly. Still, she felt her approach was right for her family. It's obvious that this mother loves her baby to the moon and back. And that she's a mother who believes so strongly in putting her child's needs first that she will go on social media to discourage everyone from seeking help or setting limits around sleep, even if it lands them in the hospital getting their meals intravenously.

After reading her comments I sat back, shocked. *How did we get this far? Is this an overcorrection from the "children are to be seen and not heard" days? A pendulum swing from the mid-twentieth century when formula feeding was encouraged so moms wouldn't spoil their babies? What must this dear mother be thinking when the fruit of her actions nearly killed her and she still thought they made sense?*

I was reminded of Luke 7:35, "Wisdom is shown to be right by the lives of those who follow it" (NLT). A complete physical breakdown is obviously not good fruit stemming from wise living, and yet after being released from the hospital, this mom jumped right back into the same old habits.

While I can't read this mother's mind, I'm guessing she must be thinking a few things—including a few thoughts I once held, BC:

- A mother's needs must come after her children's at all times, no matter which are more urgent.
- There's no way to meet both the parent's and the child's needs without anyone suffering.
- All requests for attention from the child are urgent "needs," not necessarily "wants" or "would be nice."

I believe one reason moms abandon their physical, spiritual, mental, and emotional boundaries is because they think that holding to them is selfish. And no woman trying to follow the Jesus of the Bible consciously wants to be selfish.

Consider Philippians 2:3: "Do nothing out of selfish ambition or vain conceit. Rather, in humility value others above yourselves" (NIV). When we read a verse like this, we tell ourselves, *Yes! Just as I thought! I will play Tractor-opoly for the 245th time in a row today instead of paying the bills, buying groceries, and cleaning toilets because my child needs my attention!*

But in its original language, *selfish ambition* means something other than meeting one's own needs. It implies acting selfishly for gain or putting your own interests above those of others. Its use is associated with acting out of jealousy, greed, and the desire to further your own ambitions.

And the good old Oxford dictionary defines *selfish* this way:

selfish (adj.): (of a person, action, or motive) lacking consideration for others; concerned chiefly with one's own personal profit or pleasure[1]

So as mothers of important little humans, let's ask ourselves these questions:

- Is getting enough rest so that we don't fall asleep at the wheel selfish? What about regular showers?
- Is having a few free hours a month or maybe even a week selfish?
- Is having some control over our daily routines and habits selfish?

- Is expecting an appropriate noise level in the home (so we aren't in fight-or-flight mode) selfish?
- Is it inconsiderate to ask our kids to clean up after themselves?
- Is it selfish to have kids follow the family rules so everyone lives together in peace?
- Is it selfish to give ourselves the time and space to journal or share our heart with friends?
- Is requiring our children to occasionally wait while we carry out an adult responsibility selfish?
- Is it selfish to discipline our children's behavior when society actually holds us accountable for that behavior?

Well, I know what I think. What do you think?

FINDING WIN-WINS

When parents think their choice is between caring for their children or caring for themselves, they'll normally choose their kids. Many women will stop minding their own boundaries because they think it makes them better mothers.

But that is a very black-and-white view. It's a zero-sum game in which somebody's win necessarily means the other person's loss. When speaking of parents and children, it means either the parents win or the children win.

How sad and depressing. If that's what people think, it's no wonder there's a decline in the marriage and birth rates in the United States. The messages from today's culture really make these decisions tough for us: Get married and submit to your misogynistic, patriarchal husband, or opt out of marriage and stick it to the man! Also, have kids for whom you martyr your mental and physical health until they move out in circa twenty years! (Or maybe even thirty years because good moms will always have their doors open.)

Win-lose mindsets are life-sucking. So what's the answer?

> Rather than assuming you're faced with an either-or situation, acknowledge the possibility that more options are available that you just haven't thought of yet.

Rather than assuming you're faced with an either-or situation, look for the win-win solution. How do you do that? Acknowledge the possibility that more options are available that you just haven't thought of yet. Take a step back, look for wisdom, and then start brainstorming ideas.

Win-Win Example 1

As an example, imagine you are the sleep-deprived mother I described earlier. You might think, *There must be some way I can respond to my baby's needs and still get enough sleep* and then start brainstorming ideas.

Perhaps you will feed baby for longer periods at mealtimes, resulting in longer times between feedings and giving you more time to rest. You might express milk and have your partner take over some of your baby's night feedings. You might decide to room-share so you have easy access to baby and don't have to walk down a long hall to the nursery, fully waking yourself up. Or you might give baby a pacifier to meet their nonnutritive sucking needs.

When you decide it's okay to meet your own needs, you'll be amazed at how many win-win possibilities come to mind. A great way to get started is with a popular Language of Listening® phrase that will help you go into a place of possibilities: "There must be some way to . . ."

Win-Win Example 2

Meet Joy, an introverted mama who grew up in a happy household of sisters. Somehow she's ended up with rambunctious, spicy boys who love roughhousing. A win-lose mindset would tell her she could either ignore her desire for a quiet and peaceful home or enforce strict quiet rules in the house at all times.

When Joy is honest with herself, however, she knows she could never ignore her need for quiet that long, and yet she'd be fighting an uphill battle trying to keep her boys constantly quiet.

So what does she do? She thinks of a win-win solution that allows her to get some peace and quiet and gives the kids time and space to play. She might have designated wrestling times. Or she might require that all loud play happen outdoors. Or she might decide to go outdoors whenever the loud play begins inside.

Even realizing she doesn't have to live with something she hates will energize Joy to find win-win solutions.

Win-Win Example 3

Meet Hannah, a fairly fastidious mom who doesn't like clutter. She has three little kids who love to play, and because she has generous "gift-giving love language" relatives, the kids have toys everywhere. This mess causes her a lot of stress, though she's tried to tell herself that it's fine because her kids are making memories—memories of her screaming about the mess, honestly—but she's getting better and keeps telling herself there's no moral value to having a clean house.

Whether or not that's true doesn't matter because she hates the clutter. A win-lose mindset might say she can learn to live with the mess she hates, neurotically clean up behind the kids all day, or just get rid of most of the toys.

A win-win solution, on the other hand, might be to teach the kids how to clean up and have regular tidying times throughout the day. Another win-win would be a toy rotation to keep most toys out of reach (thus making less clutter) while still allowing the kids access to plenty of toys. Another possible win-win: designating one area as the toy room, the place where messes can be made and left behind closed doors.

> Win-wins for the whole family are easy to come by when you realize they are not selfish but can be life-giving to all members of the family.

Win-wins for the whole family are easy to come by when you realize they are not selfish but can be life-giving to all members of the family. No child wants a bitter, resentful mother.

NEEDS OVER WANTS

In our home, a long hallway leads to the home office. Both my husband and I work there, and it's where I go to make important phone calls. With seven people in the house, it's often the quietest place to take care of business.

On one particular afternoon I was on an important phone call when my five-year-old came to the door. He barged in without knocking and started whining loudly about a snack. It's always about snacks.

I pointed to the phone in my hand and said, "Shhh," quietly, thinking surely he'd take the hint. Fat chance. Completely ignoring me, he spoke even louder, demanding I help him get what he wanted. My heart started beating, and I broke out into a sweat. I couldn't hear the person on the phone, and my five-year-old was talking to me as if I were a servant.

Feeling triggered, I got angry, tried to cover the phone unsuccessfully, yelled at him to leave, and then finished the call. Of course, I felt embarrassed, guilty, and awful. I was in the middle of lecturing myself about how bad a mom I was when I had a light-bulb moment. A life-changing revelation.

Without realizing it, I'd taught my kids I would drop

whatever I was doing and immediately give them what they wanted. Could this be true? Had I been so responsive to my children's wants that I had made them feel entitled to my instant attention? I started seeing evidence of the ways I'd put their momentary wants above my needs and adult responsibilities throughout our days. No wonder that, even when I really needed a minute to attend to something else, they demanded I comply immediately with their requests.

A child would wake me up from a nap because of a lost shoe. Another would come into the bathroom, staring and whining even after I said, "Please give me some privacy." They would walk right past Daddy in the kitchen to stand over me in the tub and ask for a bowl they couldn't reach.

This realization was alarming—and then it was liberating. Maybe, just maybe, ignoring what I wanted to do so I could respond to every whim of my kiddos was not producing good fruit. It was not creating well-loved, nurtured, and peaceful children. It was creating demanding, whiny, impatient kids who wouldn't give me five minutes to do anything. Including bathing.

In my effort to make sure they felt desperately loved, I had prioritized their needs and even their wants over my own. Thankfully, when I began changing my own reactions and actions, the kids learned to wait a few minutes. I continued to meet their needs, nurturing and loving them as I always had, but I dropped the guilt.

This worked. And—because miracles really do happen— they even started asking their daddy for help.

FINDING WIN-WINS

Think about the last time you were triggered by your kids demanding something from you—a snack, more playtime before bed, or a treat at the store, for example. Or think of a time when they resisted a request from you—whether to clean their room, begin their homework, or send a thank-you note. Then follow the steps below to come up with a possible win-win solution.

1. What is a common scenario in your home that makes you feel you are always "losing" and the kids are always "winning"?

2. Fill in the blanks: "There must be some way we can _____ and _____."

3. Now brainstorm win-wins.

Return to this tool whenever you're stuck on how to address a recurring issue in your home. You just might hit upon a solution that results in a win for everyone involved!

CHAPTER 5

Minding Your Own Rules

I REMEMBER THE DAY my three-year-old outsmarted me.

I was heavily pregnant with my fourth child, so I was lying down on the couch as I watched the little ones play around me in the living room. I was counting on my children listening to my instructions because I had very little energy to get up and "make them" do what I said.

My son was playing with a small ball, which he started throwing up in the air. Well, three-year-olds aren't that strong, but they also aren't that coordinated. I knew I needed to stop him before something was broken.

"Baby," I said, "we don't play with balls in the house because something will break."

Yes, I thought, very pleased with myself, *that is a rule responsible adults have.*

He stopped, looked at me briefly, and then squatted down with his ball. He said, "What bout dis, Mama?" He rolled the ball as if he were bowling. "I not bweaking anyfing!"

Honestly, it threw me for a loop. There I was lying on the couch like a beached whale with pregnancy brain while trying to maintain my parental authority. Yet I had to admit that my towheaded three-year-old had a point. If the "no playing with balls in the house" rule was designed to keep my kids from breaking anything, what was wrong with rolling one?

I felt a vague sense that I needed to forbid or enforce something. *Is rolling the same as throwing? Is he "challenging my authority" by rolling when I said no playing with balls?*

And then this: *I SHOULD STAND UP AND DO SOMETHING, OR THIS CHILD WILL END UP IN JAIL ONE DAY!*

But I didn't want to get up. First, because I didn't have the energy. Second, I honestly didn't care if he rolled the ball. I just didn't want him to break a lamp. This blanket rule "no playing with balls in the house" seemed like something every responsible parent would say, so even though I felt like I "should" make him stop, I just didn't care.

Then it hit me: He had found a way to adapt to the reason behind the rule. Breaking lamps and vases was what we wanted to avoid, and rolling the ball would prevent that from happening. He had not found a way *around* the rule so much as come up with a way to do what he wanted without breaking anything.

A win-win.

DON'T HAVE RULES YOU DON'T CARE ABOUT

Of course, throwing a ball in the house is low stakes, but this situation got me thinking about how we create and enforce rules in our home. Most of us agree that rules are necessary and important. The whole point of making them is to help create a peaceful, orderly environment so that everyone feels safe and loved and can have their needs met in appropriate and healthy ways. Yet sometimes we get "rule happy" and create new ones whenever we want to feel in charge. Then we hope our kids will simply listen and follow them.

That's not really how it works. Not only do we have to establish the rules, but we have to enforce them. Some rules are easy to insist upon because we believe in them so deeply that we couldn't *not* enforce them. Examples include restrictions on hitting, biting, or lying.

We make other rules hoping the kids will pick them up and run with them. But when they don't, we don't do anything. We create rules we don't really care about and then feel guilty when we don't enforce them. We tell the kids, "You can't do this" or "We can't do that," and then follow up with big fat nothing.

Our friends don't let kids eat snacks anywhere but the kitchen table, which sounds like a good idea. We tell the kids that, then see them eating on the living room floor, and we get that niggly feeling. The *I should do something about this* feeling. The *Other people wouldn't let this happen, so why am I?* feeling. Well, the answer is probably simple. You are letting it happen because you don't actually care. Or you kind of care, but don't have the bandwidth to do anything about it. Creating rules you won't enforce waters down your authority and confidence.

You will not enforce rules that are not important to you. Don't pretend you will. Sure, you could work on your follow-through and self-discipline as the rule keeper, but even the most self-disciplined mother doesn't end up enforcing rules she doesn't really believe are necessary. Starting now, if the kids do something you don't like, ask them to stop, but resist the urge to make a blanket rule you know you won't enforce.

> You will not enforce rules that are not important to you.

A BETTER WAY TO MAKE OUR HOUSE RULES

Mothers intuitively know how much our home's environment contributes to life happiness and maturity. We know it's up to us to teach our children all they need to know to navigate childhood and become successful adults. We want to pass on our faith and values to our children so they can live peaceful, meaningful lives that will bless others around them.

One way families teach values is through the rules they create. Some mothers love rules, and their families have a lot of them. Other mothers, not so much. Kids intuitively understand that rules are simply things we want to happen or not happen. No matter where you stand, know this: Kids love rules.

You heard me right. To a child, a rule is something that must happen all the time or must not happen all the time. Sandy Blackard, my parent coaching mentor and founder of Language of Listening®, says kids intuitively understand rules. When kids find something they like, they want to make it into a rule.

If I take the kids to get a snack at the gas station after school one time, their response is, "We are stopping to get a snack here every day!" If I cook a yummy dinner, the kids think I should make it every week. They get new toys and spontaneously make a "nobody can play with this!" rule. My kids made their own Do Not Disturb signs for their doors so nobody would come in and mess with their stuff.

Generally speaking, rules center on two main categories:

- Your values and morals
- The boundaries, limits, and preferences of family members

Let's look at these further.

Rules based on values and morals

These rules are the easiest to keep because you feel deeply about them. You don't have to convince yourself to get off the couch and enforce these because you feel so passionate about them that you don't let them slide.

Biblical commandments and principles fall under this category. I want my kids to be honest, so I don't have any trouble confronting my kids if I catch them lying. In fact, enforcing rules like that one come the most naturally to us.

We also find it easy to make rules against biting, stealing, hitting, screaming, or cheating. And we might naturally make rules that encourage kindness, loving behavior, patience, honesty, and generosity.

Surely, rules will vary across households and families based on their own day-to-day interpretation of these values, yet generally speaking it's not that challenging to stick to behavior guidelines when it comes to our deeply held values.

Rules based on your own boundaries, preferences, and limits

This area of rulemaking is a little more nuanced, but it's still important. Moms will be frazzled, strung out, and stressed whenever the pace and conditions in their homes and lives go against their own preferences. If a mom values beauty, organization, and color but her home is an untidy, ugly mess, she will be consistently unhappy in her home. If a mom is introverted yet never has any time alone, she will wither. If a mom is extroverted and never leaves the house, she is going to become despondent. If a mom needs nine hours of sleep each night but gets only five, her physical and mental health will suffer.

Disliking every part of our life is exhausting and grueling. If the environment in your home conflicts with your own personality and preferences, you will be perpetually unhappy and subconsciously looking for ways to escape your life. You'll be riding directly into the wind, meeting resistance at every turn.

That's avoidable. How do we start creating rules that put the wind at our backs? We take into account our boundaries, limits, and needs, and then we create rules around them. Let's look at some examples.

Lauren, mom of three

Lauren has a first grader, a four-year-old, and a one-year-old. She's a stay-at-home mom who is quite sensitive to her immediate environment. She likes a well-decorated and tidy home. She's also an introvert and needs downtime to stay in a good frame of mind.

Lauren has the following rules:

- Kids are not to touch decor items in the main living areas.
- Before moving on to the next thing, each child cleans up from their current activity.
- There will be no screen time until bedrooms and the living area are tidy.
- Rest time starts at 1 p.m. every day for the younger kids in the home.
- Bedtimes are strictly enforced so everyone is well-rested and parents have downtime.

These rules act as protections or scaffolding around Lauren's preferences so she's at peace in her own home environment. These rules are not moral in nature, but they are created to make the home a peaceful place for Mom—because when she is frazzled, everyone is frazzled.

Wendy, mom of two

Wendy is a homeschooling mother of a fifth grader and a fourth grader. She loves reading, spending time with her kids, exploring big ideas, and working together on creative pursuits. She is an entrepreneur with an online business, and she values hard work and ingenuity.

Wendy has the following rules:

- The morning routine starts each day at 8 a.m. sharp with the children responsible to wake themselves up and get ready.
- During the homeschool day, each child will read a book of their choosing independently for one hour before any screens are allowed.
- School days end with each child practicing some creative activity (drawing, coloring, knitting, sewing, modeling, building, coding, etc.). Only then can they play with friends in the neighborhood.
- The kids are required to carry out various age-appropriate tasks within Wendy's company so they can learn how commerce works and participate in the family business.

Because Wendy wants to raise kids who are independent, creative, and hardworking, she has created rules and routines that give her kids an opportunity to express their own interests while building skills in the areas Wendy values.

Chrissy, mom of four

Chrissy is an organized working mom, whose four kids range in age from early high school to late elementary school. She is a gentle, quiet introvert who is home-centric and doesn't like an overly full schedule. She is warm, relational, and wants a strong family bond.

Because life is already full with home and work, her rules include the following:

- Each child can participate in only one extracurricular activity or lesson at a time.
- When Mom goes into her room for quiet time and the door is closed, no one can interrupt her.
- No devices are permitted at the dinner table, and all phones are placed in a central, parent-controlled location at 8 p.m.
- Each child is responsible for writing their activities on the shared family calendar so that pickups, drop-offs, and daily routines run smoothly. If an activity isn't added to the calendar, the child will be responsible for the missed commitment.

Chrissy wants a loving, orderly home environment where everyone can thrive and bond, so she created a framework to make sure that happens without leaving her overwhelmed.

Of course, when determining your family rules, don't consider only yourself. Take into account other family members too. Your husband or children may have strong preferences, and rules can be created to help them feel safe and serene as well. This may include rules about their possessions, rooms, or time. When my kids get a new toy, for instance, they sometimes make rules for their siblings like "You have to ask me before you can play with this." If your kids are old enough to understand and contribute, hold a family meeting and get everyone's opinions on household rules. Give each child a chance to talk through any grievances and what they want to happen instead. Then work together to find some rules everyone agrees with. (Parents have the final say, of course.) Children are much more willing to follow rules they have a part in making. When we take into account our own temperaments and those of our children, we can begin to craft routines, rules, and structures around them.

Rules are to be life-giving, not life-sucking. True, sometimes we make rules in response to behaviors we want to avoid. We make rules to clarify "In this house, we don't do x." We create rules with built-in consequences ("If you do or don't do x, z happens") to help motivate children not to do certain things:

- Don't do your chores, no hanging out with friends
- Don't clean your room, no screen time
- Don't do your homework, no playtime
- Break someone else's stuff, you replace it

- Hurt someone, go apologize and repair the relationship
- Refuse to follow instructions, lose a privilege

But rules aren't made just to discourage certain behaviors; they are established to create an atmosphere for success. They are created to help our children act in positive ways. We want to set up our kids to succeed, and our rules act like scaffolding to help them thrive.

We don't let our toddlers stay up until 11 p.m. or our middle schoolers sleep with their phones. That's not because we are trying to lay down the law but because going to bed really late or with devices isn't healthy, and these behaviors would result in more difficult challenges for our kids later.

LACK OF RULES DOESN'T MAKE US MORE POSITIVE PARENTS

In today's post-postmodernist world, we tend to focus on and value behaviors that feel positive, nice, or loving to others. For many mothers, this extends to rules. They believe that rules are restrictive, controlling, and unnecessary. The idea is that moms should follow their children's lead on what should or shouldn't happen.

If a child doesn't want to do something, then surely the child knows best. If a child reacts strongly to something or demands our attention, we should just stop what we were doing. This doesn't work out well in actual practice, though. The whims, moods, and demands of her children control

Mom, who has no compass. She remains permissive and patient for as long as she can, stuffing down her own feelings and emotions. Then one day when she can't take the behavior anymore, she blows up and loses her temper.

This is what my British friend Camilla at Keeping Your Cool Parenting refers to as yo-yo parenting.[1] You go back and forth between being very permissive (because you think that's the kindest thing to do) and then launching straight into authoritarian yelling and threats (when you just can't handle your kid's behavior any longer). This is quite common and a real drag for everyone, including Mom.

And it's a self-perpetuating cycle, as we see in Amy's story. Amy prefers to grocery shop alone so she can look for the best deals on the healthiest items. However, one Saturday her husband has to work, so she brings four-year-old Sam and two-year-old Charlotte along. She tries making a game out of it by racing through the aisles, quickly looking for the lowest price before throwing that item into the cart.

Even so, the kids get hyper and excited, pointing fingers and crying, "Mommy, I want that!" They become fussy and fight with each other in the cart. When Sam tries standing in the cart to reach over and grab a box of cereal, Amy has had it.

"Samuel! Sit down right now! I better not see you move again!"

She watches as his lower lip begins to quiver and his eyes fill with tears. "Sorry, Mommy," Sam whispers.

Guilt rushes through her, and Amy feels her cheeks get warm. She quietly pushes the cart down the next aisle, where she notices the kids' eyes widen when they spot the cookie section. Despite the fact that she had already given in on several of Sam's requests for treats, she grabs a package and asks, "Would you like these, love?"

When a child acts in a way that goes against Mom's values or boundaries and Mom finally feels she needs to intervene, she doesn't really know what to do. She has no rules in place and therefore no clear repercussions for breaking them. She gets overwhelmed by her emotion—which is perfectly normal if she's been ignoring those feelings—only to let it all out on her kids. Then she feels guilty for blowing up and becomes permissive again because that's what she feels is most loving.

Not only does this make Mom feel powerless and out of control, but it also puts young children in the driver's seat of their lives when they can barely see over the wheel, are too short to touch the pedals, and have no idea where they are going.

One day the kids are happy to go to bed on time; the next day they aren't. Sometimes they listen to you when they're feeling cooperative; other times they refuse to obey when they are in a contrary mood. If they are feeling connected, they speak respectfully; if they're angry, they speak unkindly or even scream.

So what is the middle ground? Be a nurturing, loving mother while having clear boundaries and rules that reflect your own values and limits. You kiss boo-boos, listen, validate, encourage, and remain present to help your children in their day-to-day lives. You are affectionate, supportive, and always looking for ways you can support your children emotionally.

You also have clear rules with fixed consequences that reflect your own values, personality, and limits. You make sure you aren't raising kids who ignore the Bible, break the law, or act in ways that society and historical tradition agree are rude, wrong, or annoying—like screaming, being mean, hitting, lying, interrupting, insulting, etc.

You are the adult. You are responsible before both God and child protective services for how you raise your children. Letting your kids' whims and emotions rule the home means that you have abdicated your parental authority and handed it to small children who do not even understand why vegetables are better for them than kids' meals from their favorite fast-food joint.

PENDULUM PARENTING

One reason you may struggle with rules is because of the way you were parented. Pendulum parenting is when you raise your kids the polar opposite of the way you were raised, in hopes of getting a different and/or better result. If you grew up with strict parents who gave you no freedom, you may tend to be permissive. If you grew up with passive parents who had few rules, you may have craved structure and guidance and now take a stricter approach with your own kids.

Actually, the pendulum in many homes swings from permissive to authoritarian, as parents are always in search of that middle ground. The balanced approach is known as authoritative parenting.

Authoritative parenting is loosely defined as a parent having reasonable demands and high responsiveness. It means taking your children's specific needs, personalities, and emotions into account as you create and maintain family rules and boundaries that are reasonable and for everyone's good.

Remember, rules bring order

A rule is like a vehicle that gets you where you want to go. It is not the destination itself, but a way to arrive there. Rules are made to help protect our children and set them up for success. It reminds me of the Scripture on keeping the Sabbath day of rest. In Mark 2:27, Jesus says, "The Sabbath was made for man, not man for the Sabbath." We observe a day of rest because it benefits us, not because that day is in itself morally good.

> Do not be overrighteous, neither be overwise— why destroy yourself? Do not be overwicked, and do not be a fool— why die before your time? It is good to grasp the one and not let go of the other. Whoever fears God will avoid all extremes.
>
> Ecclesiastes 7:16-18, NIV

One Sabbath Jesus was going through the grainfields, and as his disciples walked along, they began to pick some heads of grain. The Pharisees said to him, "Look, why are they doing what is unlawful on the Sabbath?"

He answered, "Have you never read what David did when he and his companions were hungry and in need? In the days of Abiathar the high priest, he entered the house of God and ate the consecrated bread, which is lawful only for priests to eat. And he also gave some to his companions."

Then he said to them, "The Sabbath was made for man, not man for the Sabbath. So the Son of Man is Lord even of the Sabbath."

MARK 2:23-28, NIV

It's similar with rules. Obviously they should never lead to abuse or cruelty, but in themselves rules are neither good nor bad—they are made to encourage or prohibit actions that are. You create rules that make the home a positive place for siblings to get along. You create rules that protect people's possessions. You create rules that ensure people treat others with kindness and respect within your home.

If you find your home life is chaotic and stressful, it's time to figure out what behaviors upset you the most and start there.

🔍 DISCOVER YOUR BOUNDARY MARKERS

1. Which behaviors in your home make you the angriest?

2. What behaviors or tendencies do your children exhibit over and over again that you do not like but have given up trying to fix?

3. Fill in the blanks:

I feel resentful when _____ happens because it makes me think _____ _____.

If I could wave a magic wand and fix one problem area in my family's life, it would be _____ _____.

⚑ PUT A FLAG ON THEM!

1. I am no longer okay when my children _____ _____.

2. _____ is really keeping our family from thriving.

3. I've ignored _____ before because it felt too _____ to deal with. Now I feel _____ to address it head on.

▦ STRUCTURES, RULES, OR ROUTINES TO PROTECT YOUR BOUNDARIES

Brainstorm some possible rules.

CHAPTER 6

Minding Your Own Standards

My name is Rachel, and I'm an Aggressive Vacuumer.

For a few days I can walk around messes, dust, or piles of chaos in the house. But when it becomes too much, the inspiration to get everything in order strikes, and it strikes hard.

I start angrily vacuuming up all the crumbs, dust, crushed veggie sticks, sand, and even—fine, I'll say it—small LEGO pieces. But a funny phenomenon occurs as I make a bit of progress.

Enough is never enough.

Once I get the kitchen looking spick-and-span, the living room looks like the place all my dreams go to die. So I head there, and my vacuuming becomes even more aggressive.

I'm feeling angry! And when I feel angry, what do I want to do? I want to mood-alter, which I do by blaming someone or something else so I don't have to live with the crushing realization that I can't make my home look perfect.

My mind begins its frenzied loop:

If these kids didn't live here, the house would be nice. If I threw away all their toys, there wouldn't be a mess.
If my husband volunteered to clean every once in a while, I wouldn't have to do it all myself.
If I could follow a daily cleaning schedule, then it'd never get this bad.
If my floors were a different color, the dirt wouldn't show.
If there were room in the budget, then our house would always look company-ready.
If the house had more storage, I could hide all the junk.

Anyone or anything stopping my perfect standard from being reached is fair game.

It used to be that if anyone crossed my path during one of my aggressive vacuuming sessions, they'd regret it. I'd list five things for them to do right then, so I would no longer feel as if the house was a big landfill with vultures circling overhead.

As I worked away, my heart rate would go through the roof, I'd start sweating, and then when I was finally making progress, my fancy-pants cordless vacuum would up and die.

Goodbye, cruel world.

These days my vacuuming is less aggressive and no one

has to avoid me while I'm straightening up. It doesn't feel as heavy, I don't get into nearly as many cleaning rages, and the house is still just as tidy, or as untidy, as it ever was before.

How? I adopted realistic standards.

Instead of creating completely unrealistic ideas of what my home, life, or bank account should look like, I started zooming out. I look at my life and situation as objectively as I can and don't expect more from myself than I can deliver.

> Look at your life and situation as objectively as you can and don't expect more from yourself than you can deliver.

I live within the limits of my own energy and budget. And I don't set myself up to emotionally fail by adopting a bunch of random ideals that seem like good ideas, but that I'll never end up keeping.

STANDARDS ARE NOT BAD IN THEMSELVES

It's not that all standards are bad. It's not that we should never aim to do things well. We couldn't do that even if we wanted to. We each have preferences on how we like things done based on our personalities and temperaments. Depending on our individual giftings, we will naturally strive for excellence in some areas of life. It's how God made us.

Some people love organizing, labeling, and color-coding. Their idea of an ordered home will look different from someone else's. Another mom may love cooking and coming up with creative recipes for her family. Her idea of a good meal will look different from that of a mother who doesn't enjoy cooking.

The trouble comes when we try to excel in every area. Modern life makes everything seem possible, so we think, *Why not make sure everything in life is optimized?* This is when we get overwhelmed, overworked, and strung out.

When I consider where our standards should come from, the first place I think of is the Bible. Honestly, it's a pretty practical book. It calls us specifically to do and not do certain things. For example, from childhood, many of us are taught to be honest, patient, loving, and faithful to God. As we grow into adulthood, we read and begin to apply more of God's commands for wise living. We are to be faithful, loyal, respectful, and loving to our spouse above all, but also to our kids, our friends, and our coworkers, as well as to widows, orphans, and the impoverished. We read commands to work diligently to meet our practical responsibilities and to tithe, give, and spend wisely. Along the way, we learn to accept that the world can be cruel, people can be mean, tragedies happen, and sometimes we suffer. In these situations, we are called to forgive, be kind, remain hopeful, and believe that God is using all our struggles for good.

These are just a smattering of commands from God's Word, and when we put them all together, they take up a lot of our time and energy.

Standard optimizing procedures

These major standards alone give us enough to work on until we meet our Maker. So why, then, do we add more and more expectations on top of these? Because we can't leave well enough alone. Without realizing it, we can begin to obsess over minor issues until every part of our lives seems like it needs to be optimized or perfected. We start majoring in the minors.

We just can't seem to relax and do our best from day to day. Why is our maximum effort never good enough? We are so driven to perfection that not only do we try to be morally acceptable in the major areas of life, but we also try to maintain standards of excellence in the very minor spheres of life. Often those areas don't even matter in the grand scheme of things.

For example, we mothers decide that we must make sure our junk drawers are organized with mini compartments so everything looks tidy (even though we never use this stuff—otherwise we wouldn't keep it in our junk drawers). Our pantries should be organized, displaying food stored in glass containers with homemade labels because they look good in photos. Never mind if that requires twenty minutes of extra work each week while we put away groceries because nobody else in the house is going to keep the pantry that organized.

We should maintain a paperless, digitally organized filing system that requires scanning and sorting in folders on the cloud so we can avoid having papers pile up in our in-boxes or on our desks because visual clutter makes us more anxious. Continually scanning stacks of papers will definitely ease our anxiety, no?

Mothers who don't want their exhaustion to show on their faces must create a beauty routine that includes washing, toning, moisturizing, masking, wrinkle reducing, and spritzing with nontoxic self-tanner so they don't appear pasty, even in winter. They budget $150 a month for these products and, of course, get them through automatic home delivery.

And on and on and on.

The standards of strangers

There's a great temptation to adopt everyone else's standards as our own because they seem like good ideas—things responsible, disciplined, organized people "should" do.

On Instagram, you see images of rich women with perfectly decorated houses and kids in handwoven clothes as if they just walked out of a fairy tale set in the woods. They take nice vacations and jump up to diamond level in their MLM business—paying off six figures of debt in the process—and you think, *You know what? I'd better add that to my list.*

Never mind that you're sleeping only five hours a night, have three different types of planners to keep up with your projects, and cry yourself to sleep every night. That will all change when you finish that productivity boot camp you've been putting off.

Optimally, you and I should have six months of emergency food storage and six months of wages in our emergency fund. We should cook all meals from scratch. We should go off dairy and gluten. We should find more ways to serve our family—while also making them do more for themselves so they don't grow up entitled.

We are so privileged with our running water and electricity, not to mention automated deliveries and home robots, that we now have the time and space to find even more areas of life to excel in. To perfect.

We end up getting takeout four nights a week because we have no time to grocery shop or cook. Why? Could it be that, in addition to the demands of work, caring for loved ones, and life's normal responsibilities, we are spending hours researching the best steam mops for our particular type of hardwood or hair dryers for our particular type of hair?

We can't even make the smallest decisions now without feeling there is a "right" or "wrong" one. And who will tell us what is right or wrong in all of these minor life issues? Who knows? Google, I guess.

We create unrealistic standards in so many areas that we simply cannot live up to them. We expand our lives to include more and more, and we expect ourselves to do everything well. We become crushed under our own standards. The standards we created to help us are now our persecutors, not our friends.

WHY WE BEAT OURSELVES UP

I can remember lying in bed one night after a particularly hard day of parenting. I was thinking about my middle child, five years old at the time, and worrying about all the aspects of his future I could not control. I reminded myself I'd been failing him since he was ten months old. That's when he bit me really hard while nursing.

I screamed. He never nursed again.

All the ways in which I had been a bad mother to him flooded through my mind, along with all the things I should do now so he'd be less likely to cry, get his feelings hurt, or grow up emotionally wounded.

I was pouring out my heart to God, telling Him what an awful mother I was and asking Him to help me be better. I felt hopeless and helpless, as emo as a hormonal teenager.

And then I had a realization . . . *I do this a lot. In many areas of life.*

I beat myself up over all my failings to make sure I am doing everything as perfectly as I possibly can. I never let myself get away with anything less than "perfect."

If I'm not perfect, I reasoned, then I'm not a good Christian woman. Somehow I thought that if I didn't live up to all the standards I had created for myself, God would be disappointed in me. Without really realizing it, I'd decided a few things about meeting standards in my life.

Doing everything "right" all the time = I'm a good person

Not doing everything "right" all the time = I'm a bad person

I think many women are in a similar place.

We decide that if we are to be good women of strong character—which, of course, we want to be—then we have to excel in every area. Otherwise we are failing. Deep down we think, if we are failing, we must be lazy and undisciplined. And Christian women, of course, should not be lazy and undisciplined.

The trouble is that our lives have become complicated, overly full, and crushing. We look outside the Word of God and outside our individual personalities and limits to create these best-case scenario standards that enslave us.

We create unrealistic standards

We fail to meet them

We tell ourselves how awful we are so we'll try harder next time

We feel guilty

In theory, it is an excellent strategy for a woman who will be accepted only if she does everything right all the time. But it's really hard work—like riding that bike into the wind when you were expecting an easy ride.

Some women end up blaming God

Right now an unprecedented number of people are leaving the churches they grew up in. Deconstructing their faith. Releasing themselves from the bonds of religion and oppression. To many, following God feels stifling, overbearing, and heavy. They view Him as a daily taskmaster who is impossible to please.

But, of course, it was never possible to please God by being perfect. So where did these unrealistic and unreachable standards come from? Someone (ourselves, our parents, our leaders, etc.) created them. If we are not careful, we allow God's principles for wise living to be combined with these other standards. Where does Scripture say our home always has to pass the white-glove test or be well-decorated? Does God expect our kids to be 100 percent obedient or our food to be 100 percent organic and made from scratch? Does God actually command us to have a BMI of 20 and one year of cash in our emergency fund?

Eventually and unfortunately, many women seek to find relief and liberation from this completely unnecessary and overwhelming burden of perfection by walking away from their faith. Instead of going to God to find rest and encouragement for their wearied souls, they blame Him for setting them up to fail. Yet Jesus Himself offered us a better way:

> Are you tired? Worn out? Burned out on religion?
> Come to me. Get away with me and you'll recover
> your life. I'll show you how to take a real rest.
> Walk with me and work with me—watch how
> I do it. Learn the unforced rhythms of grace. I
> won't lay anything heavy or ill-fitting on you. Keep
> company with me and you'll learn to live freely
> and lightly.
>
> MATTHEW 11:28, MSG

He never told us we had to be perfect

The good news is this: We will never be perfect while on this earth, so we can stop beating ourselves up about it. Our job here on earth is not to make our lives or those of our children perfect. It's not to make our houses perfect. Or our careers. Or our bodies, our finances, or our life plans.

We can stop journaling about all our faults and failures and start enjoying the life we already have. If we aren't always obsessed about our "shoulds" and whether we're making progress on our goals, we will be freer to enjoy the people in front of us.

We don't have to stop caring about the issues that are important to us or stop trying to do things well, but we can recognize when we are driving ourselves into the ground. And we can offer ourselves grace.

One day years ago as I was browbeating myself about the state of my house with small kids, I had a profound insight. Sure, the house looked like a bomb had gone off right then; it was always messy in the morning when the kids were playing. If someone had come over that minute, they might have questioned my housekeeping abilities. But I realized that after I did some tidying each afternoon and again after the kids went to bed, our home looked pretty good. If someone had come over at one of those times, they'd think I was a great housekeeper.

A photograph, at any given time, is not the full picture. In fact, our lives are really not like photographs anyway; they are like videos. If someone made a time-lapse video of our living room, at some points in the day it would look embarrassingly messy, and at other times, super tidy. The average, overall, is good enough.

HOW TO HAVE STANDARDS THAT DON'T CRUSH YOU

The best way to create standards for your family is to pinpoint your values, boundaries, and preferences. There are certain areas of life you are passionate about, and you will nearly always do those well. Other areas aren't as important to you, and you can let go of the idea that you must also excel in them.

Pinpointing your values is probably pretty easy. It's all

those other little issues affecting home and family life that seem up in the air. So how do you know what to let go of?

To determine what you can live with, figure out the boundaries and limits that bring you peace. It doesn't matter what your favorite Instagrammers, YouTubers, TikTokers, bloggers, authors, or even friends can live with. It doesn't matter how robust their home systems are or how organized their pantries look. You are the one in charge of your own standards, and they should reflect your preferences and limits, not anyone else's.

> You are the one in charge of your own standards, and they should reflect your preferences and limits, not anyone else's.

Start thinking through the standards you've subconsciously adopted. Obviously, you need to keep your family safe, healthy, and fed. Outside of such necessities, you have a great deal of latitude. If you honestly don't care whether you have before and after photos of each of your children on the first and last days of school, don't stress out trying to make it happen. You don't have to have any standard at all in this area. Trust that you don't have to beat yourself up and break yourself down in order to be a better woman.

That's not how it works. It never was.

Transforming unsustainable standards into attainable ones

Instead of all-or-nothing "shoulds," we can create doable habits that lead to gracious and life-giving mindsets:

Unrealistic Standard	Realistic Standard
The house should always be clean.	I will regularly do some simple tidying routines.
I should be a perfect mom.	I will do my best to be attentive, nurturing, and patient. When I lose my temper, I will ask for forgiveness, and when I make a mistake, I'll give myself grace, ask God for wisdom, and try again tomorrow.
I need to be more organized.	I will simplify my life so there's less to organize.
I must give my children every opportunity.	Children learn valuable life skills in every situation. I don't need to create a chaotic family schedule to give them a good future.
I shouldn't feel anxious or stressed.	I will be honest about my feelings and emotions, seeking help and support from others if I need it.
I need to hustle to give my family a better life.	I will give my children a good life by being present with them rather than always being worried or working for the future.

HAS YOUR STRATEGY WORKED?

There's a reason you have tried to be the best at everything and then beaten yourself up when you failed. The question is, how well did this strategy serve you? If you beat yourself up so you'd be a hardworking woman and now you are one, then congratulations. It worked! Now you can find another gracious, more gentle way to live your life that won't run you into the ground and make you feel awful about yourself. You've earned that luxury.

Have you tried to be perfect, excel at everything, and live outside your limits for most of your life, hoping that this would make you worthy or acceptable? Did it work? Have you become perfect? No? Hmm. Well, have you become a woman who does her best? Yes? Congratulations, your strategy of self-improvement worked! Now is a good time to find a more realistic and gracious motivation strategy that doesn't make you hate your life.

Have you tried to make your life look or be picture-perfect, so you'd have the approval of others and feel good about yourself? Have you received praise and compliments from others? Is your life pretty dang good? Congratulations, it worked! Now you can be free and live your life privately without worrying about the approval of others.

We only ever have the present

We cannot waste our lives majoring on the minors. We cannot waste precious hours trying to maintain impossible standards. It seems noble and diligent, but it is wasting our lives.

The truth is this: We are not guaranteed a single day in the future.

James 4:14 (NIV) reminds us of this: "Why, you do not even know what will happen tomorrow. What is your life?

You are a mist that appears for a little while and then vanishes." And in some sense, the future never exists. We never get there. Because we are always, only, ever living in the present. And our past? It's a collection of present moments that we are no longer in. If we spend each day living for some perfect future we may have if only we get our act together, then we are building up a collection of present moments full of angst, strife, worry, anxiety, and self-inflicted browbeating.

You don't have to live like that, Mama. You can choose to let your best be good enough. That, to me, is the gold standard.

DISCOVER YOUR BOUNDARY MARKERS

1. Do you always feel as if you are never good enough or doing enough?

2. If I were more like _____, I would have my life together because she

3. I feel exhausted and weary from trying to be perfect at

⚑ PUT A FLAG ON THEM!

1. I know I have unrealistic standards when it comes to

2. I try to make everything be (or at least seem) perfect because that means that I am

3. I am willing to accept good enough in the following areas:

▦ STRUCTURES, RULES, OR ROUTINES TO PROTECT YOUR BOUNDARIES

Brainstorm how you can maintain some realistic standards without going overboard.

CHAPTER 7

Minding Your Own Friends

CANCER IS A HARD PILL TO SWALLOW. The diagnosis was like a huge lump in my throat that I couldn't get down and that threatened to choke me at every turn.

BC, the word *cancer* made me a little uncomfortable. I'd feel pity for the person who had it and try to quickly move on to discuss something else. After I was diagnosed, hearing the word or even thinking about cancer sent a cold shock wave through my body. I would go about my day doing normal things, forgetting that my own body was trying to kill me. And then suddenly I'd remember it. My heart would seem to leap out of my chest, I'd feel pain in random places, and my hands would shake. I would sit, stare off into space, and wonder what it was going to be like to meet my Maker one day.

Maybe earlier than I'd anticipated.

That happened daily for a couple of weeks shortly after my diagnosis. Then I decided to take another tack. Whether I liked it or not—and of course I hated it—I was in Club Cancer, full of unwilling members who'd had to pay their dues and were now members for life. If cancer was as devastatingly common as I knew it was, there must be a lot of people—even young mothers—who'd had it. Mothers who had been there, done that and, most importantly for my own encouragement, were still alive.

I knew that if I could talk to people who had gone through what I had and came out the other side, they would encourage me and help me face my fears. So I decided I'd try to connect with one cancer survivor a week, whether over the phone or in person—for the rest of my treatment.

It's one thing to talk to a friend who loved me and was there for me but who was now panicked they could get cancer since it had hit so close to home. If I said local doctors saw a major influx of younger women getting their first mammograms after my diagnosis, I wouldn't be exaggerating.

It's another kettle of fish, however, to have a dear friend who has gone through the same traumatic situation you are in. Who can walk and talk you through it at every stage. Who doesn't get tired of hearing your fears and who isn't trying to tie it all up with a nice bow.

My college roommate Rainy had gone through breast cancer a few years before me. She explained to me in detail, without holding anything back, what to expect from chemotherapy.

She helped prepare me for what was to come, as both a survivor and a medical professional, since she is a doctor herself.

Cancer brings with it a whole new vocabulary. At my initial appointments, my surgeon and oncologist took one look at my long, thick red hair and told me to try cold caps, which I learned were gel-pack helmets I could wear during chemotherapy to reduce blood flow to my scalp and prevent the majority of hair loss. Aside from my natural desire to keep my hair, I realized a cold cap might help to keep things as normal as possible for the kids. And as my oncologist said, strangers wouldn't stare every time I went to the store to buy tomatoes. So I froze my head for seven hours every Friday for twelve weeks.

As uncomfortable as the cold cap therapy was, it's the reason I met another friend who got me through this time. On the day of my first chemotherapy appointment, my husband and I sat in the waiting room. He was trying to remain calm and positive for me and read the instructions for the cold caps while I tried to prepare myself for what was to come.

While we sat there, a blonde woman my age came over. She was waiting to see the doctor for a follow-up appointment and introduced herself as Jessica. She told us that, at this exact same time last year, she had gone through chemotherapy for breast cancer. Like me, she'd used cold caps and had kept all her hair. We exchanged phone numbers that day, and in the months to come a deep friendship formed.

Now, along with loving family and friends, I have connected with many women who understand firsthand what

I was going through. They have lived through the initial shock and awe of receiving a cancer diagnosis. They have experienced the "how can this be my life?" feeling that comes as you watch a nurse approach you in a hazmat suit with a bag of liquid that has a skull and crossbones on it, knowing she's about to inject it into your body and that, for two days afterward, you'll have to flush the toilet twice, just to be sure none of your poisoned urine could splash on anyone's skin. They understand the sadness of lying on a bed in a pre-op room knowing that, within a few hours, you'll never be able to nurse another baby again. That one really hurt.

Along with my family, my friends got me through.

Friends and family contribute to daily happiness. And if we are happy, our families are blessed. If we are depressed, anxious, and strung out, our families wilt. We may wish it weren't true, but it is.

The more you can find ways to build yourself up, the happier and more content you are. And the happier and more content you are, the better life is. Because what it comes down to is this: Our days are our lives.

FRIENDSHIP AS LIFE SUPPORT

My situation is an extreme one, of course, but it turns out I was on to something. Support systems are critical to survival.

Real-life support systems are made up of real people who come over and bring meals every week for months. Friends who send you flowers or books and check in on you regularly. Who answer the phone when you call and let you cry. Who take care of your kids when you need to nap and who do the dishes when you just don't have the energy. They are the people down the street who look out for your yard, or the other school moms who help you with drop-offs and pickups. The people at church who stop to ask how you are because they look into your eyes and see that you aren't fine.

If asking for help makes us feel ashamed or inadequate, we will resist doing it. If asking for help feels like a burden lifted, we will do it freely. Often we have people around us who want to help but don't know what to do until we share our needs.

Kelly A. Turner's book *Radical Remission* and Chris Wark's book *Chris Beat Cancer* both give detailed accounts of studies showing that robust support systems, loving family, and friends actually prolong life in terminal cancer patients compared to those who feel alone, lonely, and depressed.[1] When we are weary, worn out, and beyond our limits, one of our most life-giving survival strategies can be leaning on friends.

Smartphones make us present but absent parents

BC I spent a lot of time surfing Instagram. When the house got chaotic and the kids were loud and I felt unmotivated, I'd often escape into my room or closet to scroll the site, catching up on the perfect lives of random strangers—where they were going, what they were doing, what their kids were wearing, and how tidy their houses were. It never left me encouraged or relaxed, though. In fact, it did the opposite. It left me feeling not good enough, not skinny enough, not pretty enough, and not rich enough. *How does she pose like that so her hip sticks out and her waist looks tiny? Will I ever be thin again after my fifth child?*

Deep thoughts.

Still, I kept going back like a dog to its own vomit (see Proverbs 26:11).

After my diagnosis, I instantly dropped Instagram like the bad habit it was for me. I no longer cared about these strangers' lives. Who cared about the latest fashion trend when I might die before I hit forty?

All the energy I'd put into my phone was freed up. Now that I no longer focused on the lives of strangers, what did I have time for? I could focus on my own people—my own relationships, my own kids. Eventually, AC, I learned to use Instagram in a more active way by signing on to post, respond to comments, or check out another account directly, and then closing the app. I no longer aimlessly scroll the feed, constantly refreshing again. Because of how freeing life is without it, returning to the endless scroll isn't even a temptation.

An article I wrote to encourage other moms to pay attention to their own technology use, "The Dangers of Present but Absent Parenting," became one of my most viral posts. I wrote another post that went viral about a habit we start while nursing our babies—endless scrolling—that carries on for years.[2] Both posts reflect the reality of many mothers I hear from who grew up with parents who were there, but not there. Emotionally absent, distant, or distracted.

Our phones do this to us if we aren't careful. They keep us distracted and unfocused, and we know it. Instead of making life more convenient or easier, our phones attract our focus like a porch light attracts moths. We may follow or like posts, statuses, or videos from acquaintances while rarely seeing our real-life friends.

In those early years of child-rearing, it is easy to shift our social lives from enriching in-person interactions to online ones that don't offer nearly the same benefits. In fact, the more time we spend online, the more depressed, anxious, and lonely we get. Because being online is not being present.

Often, it's a distraction and an escape. Don't wait for a diagnosis like I did before making changes that enrich your life. Time is the one resource you cannot get back. You can spend it, but it never multiplies. Nobody on their deathbed is happy they spent a lot of time on their phone. In fact, around ten years ago my friend's elderly grandfather said something interesting on his deathbed. While he was lying there quietly, my friend asked what he was thinking about. I'm sure he was expecting to hear about a precious memory or maybe even a regret. Instead his grandfather said he was thinking of how computers had ruined the world. On some days, I agree with him.

If you find yourself grabbing your phone and scrolling mindlessly throughout the day, here are some ways to help you break free of that.

Stop carrying your phone around with you. Choose a central hub for your phone, and leave it there at all times unless you need to use it for something specific.

Set aside times to use your phone guilt-free. After you put your kids down for naps or bedtime, or when they are otherwise occupied, you might choose to unwind with your phone for a predetermined amount of time.

Create boundaries around your phone use. You can download apps that help you track time spent on certain apps or even block access to those apps during specific times.

If you tend to scroll whenever you get bored, carry a book around in your bag instead. This will help you break the habit of constantly reaching for your device.

Instead of scrolling when you have to wait in line while out, strike up a conversation with someone. People all need connection these days, and you may have a rich interaction that stays with you for days.

First Thessalonians 4:11 says: "Make it your ambition to lead a quiet life: You should mind your own business and work with your hands" (NIV). What is my business? My family, my home, my work, my church, my friends. If I'm writing captions for a post in my head or obsessively following the lives of total strangers, I am not focused on my own life. I'm focused on what others think about my life. And that's a one-way ticket to bondage.

Connected but lonely

Thanks to the internet, we are more connected than ever before, but interestingly enough, we are also lonelier. Funny how that works. The more we live online, the less we live in the here and now. The less we live in the present, the more anxious and depressed we feel.

> If I'm obsessively following the lives of total strangers, I am not focused on my own life. I'm focused on what others think about my life.

But this isn't because we are bad mothers.

We are often caring for small children at home with little social interaction. The days are long, but the years are short. Playdates often seem like more trouble than they're worth. Running errands or getting coffee with friends when you have three kids three and under? Fat chance. Grocery delivery and the Keurig will do.

Days go by without shaving or doing our hair; after all, why would we want to spend two hours getting ready to spend one hour in a coffee shop in fight-or-flight because our toddler won't sit still just so we can attempt to have an adult conversation?

Also, many women live far from their own families. It can feel exhausting to put roots into an area or even just put yourself out there. Who knows how long it will be before you move again? And if you're introverted, it may feel like too much effort for too little gain. It can take months or even years to make deep friendships, so of course it's easier to message existing friends even if they live states away.

Sometimes our daily lives are so full that we don't think we even have time for people outside our household. There's work and then all the cooking, chores, and bedtime routines.

We're in survival mode, just trying to stay afloat.

Then to top it all off, most people's focus has shifted away from local issues. We are obsessed with national politics and don't know who our town's mayor is. We chat with strangers in online mom groups from across the country, but we haven't met our neighbors in similar life stages. We stream sermons from pastors in another state and barely even talk to our own.

While none of this is necessarily bad or good, in a moral sense, it does have effects. We become disconnected from the place and people where we are actually living our daily life—including, at times, our own kids!

REAL-LIFE RELATIONSHIPS MAKE LIFE WORTH LIVING

When we are in the busy years of motherhood, life can feel so overwhelming. We barely make it to the end of the day without bursting into tears, and it feels like reaching out to others takes too much energy. And maybe it does. But it can also give us energy, relief, and encouragement to keep going.

Social support systems have benefits that are so far-reaching they actually prolong life. Such "villages" used to be common. Now, our villages are spread out across the country and maybe even the world, and we chat with them on our phones. And that's okay too. But not if that takes the place of real-life relationships.

I follow a popular author who seems to have the most amazing friends and family around her. She frequently posts about those in her life who always seem to show up when she needs them. They make meals. They watch her kids. They buy her thoughtful gifts and are there when she needs a shoulder to cry on. They listen and give advice at just the right times.

Once I saw a comment on one of her threads that gave me a light-bulb moment. The person said something like "I'm so glad you have amazing friends and family, but the rest of us don't, so this all feels a bit braggy."

Initially, I kind of agreed, but then I thought, *Wait a minute . . . this is a genius strategy.* It goes without saying the author doesn't do this on purpose in a manipulative way, but she is so vulnerable about her moods and needs that her people show up. Then when they do, she brags about how great her friends and family are. And this keeps the cycle going.

The cycle of asking for help and receiving that help. Of loving others and being loved. Of being vulnerable and in relationship with people who live in your actual town. Who you can call if you need physical, emotional, or mental help.

Back when we lived in Australia, I had three kids two and under and my house felt out of control, so I called a super tidy and organized friend for help. She showed up with her best cleaning supplies. She helped me clean our townhome from top to bottom. Even when I wanted to quit because I thought it was good enough, she set it all to right. With joy and a smile. It was her pleasure to help, and she repeatedly thanked me for asking her over. I couldn't believe she was thankful that I'd asked her to come clean my toilets, but she was.

I saw the power of local, in-person community years ago, just before I moved to Italy to find myself after college. My church in southern Florida reached out to a single mother who lived with her kids in a nearly condemned mobile home. The floor was caving in, and she was struggling to meet her bills month to month. Our church arranged a trip to Puerto Rico for her and her kids so they could visit family while people from the church fixed as many issues within her home as possible.

When the volunteers went into her home, what they found was both uplifting and convicting. Parts of the home were falling apart, and you were really tempted to pity them. Until you looked at their walls. They were dotted with encouraging pictures and Scripture verses like "As for me and my house, we will serve the LORD" and "Godliness with contentment is great gain."[3]

A fascinating thing happened as others in the church heard about the project. More and more volunteers—more than could fit in her tiny house—showed up to help. Many of them—myself included—had no actual skills to contribute but wanted to experience the purpose and meaning that come from actively helping others. No one wanted credit; they wanted to serve and love simply for the joy of doing it. And that's how we are made. Living online instead of living in real life robs you of the joy and privilege of helping others personally and also getting personal help.

There is joy and purpose in giving, serving, and loving others. In fact, it's how the Bible calls us to live. But how can we do that if we don't know what others are going through? And how will we ever know what others are going through if we are just scrolling strangers on Insta? If others in our neighborhood, town, or church don't know us, we don't know them either.

WAYS TO BUILD FRIENDSHIPS AND SUPPORT SYSTEMS

There is nothing more discouraging than feeling alone— alone in your struggle, alone in your situation, alone in your home. When you have babies, toddlers, and preschoolers, the days are so long. And while the little ones can give amazing hugs and cuddles, you may often feel starved for grown-up conversation.

Caring for our little ones takes up most of our time and energy. It's overwhelming. It's exhausting. But it's in these years that we'd most benefit from help, support, and friend-ship. And because most of us live life online instead of in the local community, we don't even know how to get it.

As I've wrestled with that dilemma, I've discovered a few approaches that have led to rich friendships.

Think outside the age box

One friend who helped me through cancer treatment, Sheryl, is about ten years older than me. She went through breast cancer when she was my age. And another two times since then. When I felt scared or panicked, I could reach out to her. Sheryl would listen—sometimes come over—and point me back to the Lord. She was someone I could rely on and reach out to when I felt bad. Her support was life-giving.

Friends don't have to be your same age or in the same life stage. In fact, if you're a mom of young kids, it may be hard to find a mom your age for support because you are both likely to be strung out and exhausted.

This is a great time to make friendships with older women who don't have little ones underfoot. They have more time and remember the challenges of the stage you are in. These women can offer their perspective, wisdom, and practical help. Seek them out in your church. Be vulnerable about your struggles.

Think local first

When you are going through something and need to talk with someone, start locally. Instead of immediately reaching out to a friend across the country, reach out to someone near you, someone you may run into this week.

Forget about how your house looks, and invite that person over. Schedule the visit for when your little ones are down for a nap so you can concentrate on your time together. Or invite this person over after the kids are in bed. If you don't purposefully cultivate relationships with people near you, you won't have any.

When our schedule permits, we'll invite a family over for dinner and a swim. We choose an easy meal and let the kids play outside so there's no mess to clean up later. Thinking easy instead of elaborate means it'll actually happen.

Be real

People who are real feel safe to others. Even if you don't agree with everything they do or say, you can relax when you're with them. Be this type of person. Forget about looking good, sounding good, or performing. That is vanity and doesn't fool anyone.

If you're sad, be sad. If you're angry, be angry. If you're discouraged, ask for encouragement. If you want to cry, cry. If you are about to drown, ask someone to throw you a life preserver.

Pray you'll run into someone who can encourage you. Believe that God hears your prayers and answers them. If you don't think prayer works, it's because you haven't done it enough. Scripture says, "You do not have, because you do not ask" (James 4:2). So ask.

Find a church or a mom's group. If you behave authentically, you'll attract others who do the same. Go to your pastor or small group leader and say, "I can't take it anymore. Do you know anyone who might be able to help me this week?" Be specific. You need help; this isn't the time to hold back. When you find someone with the desire to help, talk to them for as long as you can. Tell the kids to be quiet and wait; they will be okay. They will learn patience.

Be a friend to have a friend

If all else fails and you feel disconnected, love others first. Find out who needs help in your area, and give it to them. Look for a mother who is worn out, and make or bring her some food.

> If all else fails and you feel disconnected, love others first. Find out who needs help in your area, and give it to them.

If you know a family in your church or neighborhood that is struggling financially and you are not, pay some of their bills anonymously. Get them gift cards to the grocery store. If you don't currently have extra funds, you can at least drop off an encouraging note. If you see something you know would lift someone's spirits, bring it to them. Give time, attention, and love to others. Even if they don't pay you back immediately—or ever—you will feel encouraged.

You will feel connected. You will feel alive. You will truly understand on a deeper level that it is better to give than to receive (see Acts 20:35), and in giving, you will receive some balm for your weary soul.

🔎 DISCOVER YOUR BOUNDARY MARKERS

1. Are you lonely during your current season of life? Name some specific reasons why.

2. Do you have life-giving friendships? Do these friends live locally, or are they spread out?

3. What are the biggest barriers in your life to having thriving, life-giving friendships?

⚑ PUT A FLAG ON THEM!

1. When I think of getting together with my friends, I feel

2. The thought of having people over to our house makes me feel

3. There are _____ people in my life whom I can call if I feel on edge, overwhelmed, or sad. This number [circle one] is / is not enough for me.

▦ STRUCTURES, RULES, OR ROUTINES TO PROTECT YOUR BOUNDARIES

1. My phone is a [circle one] means of communication / method of distraction. I will put the following strategy in place to keep me from being constantly tied to my phone:

2. In order to cultivate my real-life friendships, I will prioritize

3. I can be a good friend to those around me by regularly

4. While having young children is a legitimate reason to be less social, I will not use it as an excuse to remain lonely. Instead I will

CHAPTER 8

Minding Your Own Emotions

My husband and I met while studying at Ellel Ministries UK, a Christian ministry center just outside of London. I had just finished my master's degree and was ready to take on the world for God and rescue everyone in the process. But I decided that before I could do that, I needed some ministry training.

Early on there was a class session I will never forget. Jill Southern, who led the ministry center then, gave such a great illustration of my entire life that I was shocked. Could this one principle explain why I hardly ever cried and then when I did start crying, I couldn't stop? Might it also explain why I seemed like a perfectly normal, reasonable person until something small triggered me and I exploded with rage, panic, or hysteria?

After I got married and became a mother, more and more this principle proved true in my life. Things would trigger me, and I'd react disproportionately to what was happening. But after hearing this illustration, I knew why I wasn't the calm, cool, and collected woman I wanted to be. I knew why I went into a panic over stuff that didn't really matter in the grand scheme of life.

Because I had a full and overflowing emotional basement.

YOUR EMOTIONAL BASEMENT

Think of yourself like a modest ranch-style home.

There are a few bedrooms, bathrooms, a living room, a kitchen, and a basement. The main level is lovely, cozy, and safe with pretty furnishings and art. And the basement, well, that's where the ugly stuff is stored and stuffed.

Our emotional basement is where we shove all the emotions and feelings we don't want to look at. It's the place we put the things we aren't ready to deal with and don't like. And throwing everything down there works for a good long while because, after all, basements are pretty large.

> Our emotional basement is where we shove all the emotions and feelings we don't want to look at.

That time as a child when something ugly was said about you? Stuff it in the basement.

Felt unloved or neglected as a child? Put it in the basement. Failed a grade? Basement. Bullied and called names at school? Way down in the basement.

Had a college boyfriend who cheated on or broke up with you? Basement. Friend spreading rumors? Basement. Pain and suffering from infertility or loss of a child? Deep in the basement. Humiliation and shame from unwise or embarrassing choices? Basement.

Stuffing overwhelming feelings in your emotional basement is an effective strategy to keep ugly, unwieldy, or unpleasant things hidden, so they don't ruin your lovely house. You just stuff them down. You aren't sure what to do with uncomfortable feelings and don't want others to see the less-than-presentable parts, so you bury them out of sight. But out of sight is not, unfortunately, out of mind.

Burying the ugly parts of life is very clever—until the emotional basement gets full. And then it gets harder and harder to shove things into it. You feel an emotion you want to stuff, but as soon as you open the door to the basement, you notice that the junk has filled the entire room and is now creeping up the stairs, trying to burst out the door. In fact, trying to stuff one more uncomfortable emotion down causes fifty-five other things to fall out onto the floor around you.

Now your excellent strategy of stuffing things in your emotional basement stops working because all the unsightly things down there start overflowing into the home—where real life happens. Soon you can't walk anywhere without running into the stuff you'd rather stash away. And you can't even pretend it's pretty because it also stinks.

When the emotional basement is overflowing, it seems as if every single thing you stuffed down previously has to be dealt with immediately. It all seems to command attention *now* because there's nowhere to put it.

This is how you end up feeling intense emotions out of proportion to the current situation. You don't just have the pain of one heartache; you have the pain stemming from about 2,345 heartaches there, exploding out of the basement onto your nice rug in the hallway. I remember one time coming home and looking forward to eating a leftover ham biscuit in the refrigerator, only to find it had already been eaten. I sat down on the kitchen floor and cried for twenty minutes.

When your emotional basement is full, you don't have just one worry about a particular situation; you have worry from all the other similar situations there. When you trip over it, you're reminded that you do, in fact, have a lot to worry about. A lifetime's worth of worries, in fact.

You thought you could take life's inevitable annoyances in stride. You might have thought that repressing your emotions was helpful in the moment, but the truth is that your feelings never really went away. Now the slightest problem sets you off. One misbehavior from your kids, and you explode. One broken dish, and you feel the pain of every broken relationship you've experienced. A child talks back, and you feel the sting of all the times someone spoke disrespectfully or rudely to you. Even minor situations take on extreme significance.

The more you have stuffed down over the years, the more your emotions explode out sideways. Before you know it, your emotions begin taking over your life.

CONTENTMENT MAY NOT BE A CURE-ALL, BUT IT WILL HELP YOU SURVIVE ALL

We often believe that suppressing our feelings or, worse, beating ourselves up for having these feelings, is both disciplined and righteous. But the fact is that not allowing ourselves to feel what we already feel creates dissonance in the body and causes further harm. Sometimes we need to wail and cry and offload our feelings, like David did in Psalm 109. He says some shocking things there about those who'd hurt him, and he ends by praising God. Even with this, he's still a man after God's own heart:

> May those curses become the LORD's punishment
> for my accusers who speak evil of me.
> But deal well with me, O Sovereign LORD,
> for the sake of your own reputation!
> Rescue me
> because you are so faithful and good.
> For I am poor and needy,
> and my heart is full of pain.
> I am fading like a shadow at dusk;
> I am brushed off like a locust.
> My knees are weak from fasting,

and I am skin and bones.
I am a joke to people everywhere;
    when they see me, they shake their heads in scorn.
Help me, O LORD my God!
    Save me because of your unfailing love.

PSALM 109:20-26, NLT

Never allowing ourselves to feel hard emotions does not make us more righteous; it makes us more anxious and depressed. Because the emotions are still there—they are simply buried.

How buried emotions affect our health

After I was diagnosed with cancer, I began noticing a lot of functional medicine practitioners emphasizing the role of emotions in our health. In fact, many went so far as to suggest that repressed emotions were the single most common contributing factor of cancer in the patients they'd seen.

Needless to say, I decided crying was a great idea at that point.

In very simple terms, the theory goes like this: Deep, unexpressed, out-of-control pain is highly stressful to the body, suppressing the immune system and resulting in out-of-control cell growth.[1] Obviously, there are a variety of factors that lead to cancer diagnosis, many of which are not related to lifestyle, but this was compelling to me. It rang true for me.

I started asking around and was shocked to find I wasn't alone. Everyone I knew who'd been diagnosed with cancer at some point had either a traumatic childhood or some traumatic event within a few years of their diagnosis. Lots of pain, lots of trauma, lots of heartbreak. Sure, this was only my small sample of people, but everywhere I looked, this same scenario presented itself.

I'm not saying that being happy will prevent or cure cancer, but we do know that a history of repressed emotions and pain creates stress in our bodies. And of course, stress lowers our immunity. When our immunity is lowered, we are susceptible to any number of things in our bodies breaking down.

Each of us is not just a body, but spirit, soul, and body (see 1 Thessalonians 5:23). And these parts are connected and cannot be separated. We cannot be in horrible emotional health yet in excellent physical health. In fact, even studies within epigenetics support this. When we look at the effect of behavior and environment on gene expression, there is evidence that trauma and pain affect our genes and can be passed on in utero.[2]

How buried emotions affect our parenting

Hair-trigger tempers, explosions, and yelling are obvious ways our emotions come out in our parenting. We may feel out of control and have to do some relationship repair with our kids after our outbursts.

But there are less obvious ways our buried emotions affect how we parent. When we are a bundle of nerves and emotions, we are also less objective. Instead of seeing things neutrally, we take others' choices personally. Because we never allowed ourselves to "selfishly" feel our emotions, we inadvertently make everything that happens about us.

Picture this scenario: Your preschooler uses one of your favorite coffee mugs, which she accidently drops and breaks. You can react in a couple of different ways:

RESPONSE #1: *My child wasn't careful, and the mug broke. I will put unbreakable glasses within her reach so next time she will use them, not my mugs.*

RESPONSE #2: *My child was reckless, as always, and broke my mug. People are never careful with my things, which always end up broken or destroyed.*

The first response leaves room for you to admit your annoyance, but it is constructive rather than explosive. The second response takes one event—a broken mug—and combines your response with a lot of other feelings in your emotional basement. Not surprisingly, then, a broken mug triggers a cascade of anger.

If our emotional basements are full, even the slightest mistake by our children can send us into emotional overdrive, and we blame them for what feels like a lifetime's worth of woes.

In chapter 5, we talked about pendulum parenting—the tendency we have to parent in the exact opposite way that our parents raised us. Moms who have a lot of emotional pain and heartache often end up engaging in pendulum parenting, whether in just a few or many areas of family life. It's not a conscious choice, but it becomes obvious to many moms who observe their own parenting patterns.

We all likely engage in pendulum parenting to some degree, but for those with a stuffed emotional basement, it becomes a way of life. Their unprocessed and unresolved pain screams out that the way they were parented was all wrong, so they need to do it differently. Let me give you an example.

Ashley, a mother of three, wasn't allowed to share her emotions much as a child. When she tried to express how she felt, her parents redirected her, trying to distract her from how she was feeling. They didn't offer her much comfort; they just pushed her to get over it. Now, as a mother, Ashley heavily prioritizes her children's emotions in her decision-making.

She is always responsive to their feelings and wants to make a safe and secure home for her children. The problem is that Ashley is afraid to set any limits around the way her children express their emotions. She doesn't want them to have their own stuffed basements, so she lets them yell, scream, rant, and throw tantrums both at home and in public. As a child, she wasn't able to feel what she felt and then move on; now her own children's emotions are allowed free rein. Ashley often feels at the mercy of their moods. Without her realizing it, her unwillingness to set limits on the way her children express themselves stems from her desire to avoid repeating her own past.

Pendulum parenting can manifest in different ways, but the key is realizing that our stuffed emotional basement affects the choices we make as parents. And often we make choices we don't even like, just to avoid having to feel all those overflowing feelings.

EMPTYING THE EMOTIONAL BASEMENT

I wish there were a quick way to empty and get rid of all that emotional baggage. If you have endured trauma, betrayal, or abuse of any kind, counseling or other outside help may be critical to sorting through all that has been sent your way. But sometimes, if the junk mostly consists of small slights and hurt feelings you just haven't wanted to deal with, you may find that a little forgiveness (of others and yourself) goes a long way. Whether you face those feelings solo or with someone else's help, forgiveness will clear some of the baggage that's weighing you down. After all, we've all heard the saying that unforgiveness is like drinking poison and waiting for the other person to die.

> Be kind to one another, tenderhearted, forgiving one another, as God in Christ forgave you.
>
> Ephesians 4:32

Forgiveness, a biblical command, is healing. Releasing others from your own form of justice and giving that responsibility to God will help you feel lighter and freer as you let go of bitterness and resentment.

Acknowledging deep regret over our own choices could

bring great relief too. Repentance can also free us from a lot of our baggage.

But these changes don't happen overnight. More often than not, emptying that emotional basement is daily work: We do it one situation or emotion at a time, as something else starts to explode out of the basement. When we get a little braver, we venture downstairs and begin going through things, figuring out what to keep and what to throw away.

Eventually, you are able to group similar feelings and experiences. You realize that it's no wonder one tiny incident brings a ton of self-doubt. You've got a bunch of insecurity stuffed in the basement. Of course, this is where you might decide it's time to seek counseling, which can help you unpack and deal with all the feelings you've been stuffing down.

Counseling is very accessible these days and available at nearly every budget.[3] If you have a bad taste in your mouth about it, you just haven't found a good counselor yet. Keep looking.

Bottom line: When the kids spill their milk, there's no need to explode like the world is ending if you don't have to. And you don't have to.

Strong emotions are advisors, not masters

As you start emptying your emotional basement, you will gradually begin to see emotions in a new light—not as garbage to stuff down, but as alerts. Emotions are advisors that guide us. When you are in an emotionally healthy place, you pay attention to your feelings and then engage your own brainpower, wisdom, and values to make decisions.

In other words, you recognize that you have strong reactions for a reason. What is it? What's going on down there in your heart or mind? Emotions can serve to help us live in the present, face our feelings, forgive or change our current behaviors, and live more wholly and peacefully. Once we feel safe to feel our feelings, we will no longer need to stuff them down.

On the other hand, there's an age-old proverb about emotions that goes like this: *Emotions are excellent servants, but bad masters.* They become ruthless commanders when they are so strong and overwhelming that they control our every move. Maybe a friend shows up twenty minutes late for a playdate without calling, and instead of simply saying, "So glad you're here! If you're running late next time, could you text to let me know?" you fume inside and give her the silent treatment.

To break out of this cycle, we have to begin emptying our own emotional basements with care. These feelings may lead us to places of deep hurt within ourselves. Feelings and emotions may overcome us for a time, but then they will pass. Instead of stuffing and avoiding, which lead to anxiety and stress, we need to be kind to ourselves, allowing ourselves to feel whatever we feel and let it go. Prayerfully, we can invite people in our lives to help us, just like on moving day when we call up our friends to assist us in loading the trucks.

As we address these deep places of pain and heartache, we find our emotions stop taking over our lives at the drop of a hat. We aren't so likely to lose our tempers on our children and yell. When our kids behave in typical childish ways, we don't blame them for making our lives miserable. When our buried emotions aren't exploding into every area of our lives, we are more calm, more at peace, and happier.

Our emotions stop controlling our every move.

Don't beat yourself up, just get to the root

Many moms these days feel unhappy, stressed, and anxious—and then feel guilty for feeling unhappy. They get mad at themselves, believing they "can't do anything right," and this leaves them feeling bitter on top of it all. This heaping pile of feelings on top of buried emotions makes them want to blow it all up and escape their own lives.

If that describes you, it's time to break the self-condemnation cycle and give yourself some grace.

The key is to get to the root of your emotions rather than stuffing the symptoms. The situation that set you off was probably not the real issue. The actual fuse is whatever happened that caused you to allow the emotions to overflow in your basement in the first place. As you begin to get curious about what is buried under there, you can invite counselors, pastors, and friends to help you carefully empty that emotional basement so your home isn't overrun with baggage, stuffed full of things done to you and things you've done. Having others help you work through it all carefully and prayerfully is the path to healing, enabling you to forgive others and yourself, to take responsibility for your own part, and to find healing.

As you begin emptying your emotional basement and learn to view your emotions in a healthy way, give yourself some grace. You are dealing with a lifetime's worth of emotions, and there's no need to heap guilt on yourself for not being perfect at clearing it away.

You can never get where you want to go if you don't accept the reality of where you're at. Imagine entering a fake starting address into your GPS and expecting to get to your destination. The directions wouldn't make any sense.

As you try to navigate all of your emotions, stop beating yourself up. There is no perfectly right way to do most anything so cut yourself some slack. Many mothers are downright horrible to themselves. They don't see falling down as just a random mistake; they fall down on the ground and then start banging their head on the floor, just to punish themselves because they fell down in the first place.

Imagine if you treated your neighbor as you treat yourself.

Jesus replied, "'You must love the LORD your God with all your heart, all your soul, and all your mind.' This is the first and greatest commandment. A second is equally important: 'Love your neighbor as yourself.' The entire law and all the demands of the prophets are based on these two commandments."
MATTHEW 22:37-40 (NLT)

If we loved our neighbor as we love ourselves, most of us would tell her she is doing a bad job at life. We'd tell her she should put on some real clothes, not stretchy pants, and do a little more with her hair.

We'd say that, actually, if she were more self-disciplined, health conscious, and consistent, she would be back in her prepregnancy clothes already instead of blaming the extra weight on her baby even years later. We would point out all the bulges, wrinkles, cellulite, and blemishes she has.

When she was going through a hard time, we'd tell her to stop whining and crying because it wouldn't change anything. We would look her in the eye and tell her to get over it and muscle through her misery. We'd remind her that other people in the world have much worse problems, so she should be ashamed of herself for feeling bad.

If we loved our neighbor as we love ourselves, we'd tell her she's a bad mom. And we'd say her house is never clean enough, her bank account never large enough, and her to-do list never complete enough.

If we loved all our neighbors as we love ourselves, we would be the most hated woman on the block.

The next time you're tempted to put yourself down, try treating yourself with the same gentleness you'd offer a friend instead. It might just change your life.

○ DISCOVER YOUR BOUNDARY MARKERS

1. I tend to explode, yell, or feel very triggered much more than the situation warrants when my children

2. I think this is because

3. All signs point to the likelihood that I [circle one] have / don't have a full emotional basement.

4. When I think about feeling all my buried feelings, I immediately want to

⚑ PUT A FLAG ON THEM!

1. I get really angry or frustrated when

2. I feel bitter and resentful when

3. I feel worried or fearful when

4. I zone out or become emotionally distant when

▥ STRUCTURES, RULES, OR ROUTINES TO PROTECT YOUR BOUNDARIES

1. Research different calming strategies you can keep in your toolbox to bring yourself back to reality when you feel overwhelmed. These may include breathing exercises, putting both feet on the floor, swishing saliva in your mouth (yes, I'm not kidding!), practicing muscle relaxation, and more.

2. Grab a journal and make it a place to unload your emotional basement. Write down your feelings and use Scriptures or draw pictures to help express what you're feeling. Get it out; don't keep it in.

3. Consider finding a friend, pastor, counselor, or support group if you have a lot of baggage in your emotional basement. Remember, support is life-giving.

CHAPTER 9

Minding Your Own Daily Care

I'LL NEVER FORGET those first months with a newborn baby. It was an intense time of nurture and care.

Infants are so tiny, soft, and helpless. They have the cutest sneezes and make the sweetest faces. They can't do anything for themselves except feed and sleep. And even those are struggles for some babies.

Babies can't understand the words "I love you" or appreciate the cozy, personalized decorations in the nursery. They don't care about the expensive keepsake dolls we bought and can't even safely sleep with the handmade bedding made by relatives yet.

Our hearts explode with love, affection, and tenderness for our newborns, and it shows in the way we care for them day in and day out.

We don't let them stay in their soiled diapers; we keep them dry and clean. If they are cold or warm, we add or remove a blanket. We feed them purposefully and then spend as much time as we need burping them to prevent any gas pains later. We meticulously wash away any spit-up that somehow finds itself in their lovely skin folds.

We carefully wash and care for our baby's skin. We choose soft onesies, swaddles, and receiving blankets, beaming with joy as we look at our babies bundled up so cutely. Sometimes we change their outfit a few times a day just to make sure we get to use all the clothes we were gifted.

When babies cry, we offer whatever comfort best suits their needs. If they wail from hunger, we feed them. If they cry from tiredness, we settle them down so they can fall asleep. If they fuss because of a wet or dirty diaper, we change it. If they cry from overstimulation (too many people touching or talking or making faces), we remove them from that environment. If we've done everything we can think of and our babies are still crying, we simply comfort them through their distress.

In short, we treat babies exactly the opposite of how we treat ourselves.

These simple acts (hygiene, dressing, eating well, sleeping, etc.) move way down our list of priorities for ourselves. Not only do they seem unimportant, but sometimes we decide they are no longer even necessary.

After all, babies, toddlers, and preschoolers require 24-7 care and attention. Some things have to go. More so than during any other season in life, we must major on the majors and minor on the minors.

But now is a good time to ask ourselves . . . are these acts of self-care really minor?

WHEN IT DOESN'T FEEL WORTH IT

I used to think that taking care of myself meant getting a monthly manicure. I would choose a time when my husband could be home. I'd then feed the baby and immediately jump in the car to maximize every single second before she needed to be fed again.

With our first couple of babies, we hadn't thought to introduce a bottle early enough, so they would not take one. They'd simply scream until Mommy was available. You can imagine how pleasant that was. I was a little bit pleased at their loyalty, but mostly I felt trapped because I could never go anywhere for more than two and a half to three hours.

When we lived in Australia, we had an old black Vauxhall Astra sedan we'd bought from a friend for peanuts. It was a manual, aka a stick shift. Unfortunately for me, all the streets in our neighborhood had roundabouts instead of good ole-fashioned stop signs. Is your heart racing just reading that? Mine is as I remember it.

Driving a manual put me into fight-or-flight mode. Navigating roundabouts made it worse. And knowing I had approximately three hours (if I was lucky) to get back before the baby started screaming made my drive straight to the shopping center even more fraught with emotion.

It took twenty minutes to get to the mall even though it was only a few miles away because, you know, the suburbs. I'd power walk from the parking lot to the nail salon and pray the wait wasn't long. Instead of relaxing and enjoying this mini luxury, I'd watch the clock or check my phone the whole time I was getting my nails done. *Is the baby okay? Why is this taking so long?*

When my nails were finished, I'd run a couple of errands and then race back to the car to get home. Usually before I even reached our driveway, I'd get a call that the baby was screaming for me, which meant the remaining minutes were filled with guilt, anxiety, and tears.

I'd been trying to enjoy a little treat but ended up more stressed than I would have been staring at ugly nails.

TREATING YOURSELF VS. TAKING CARE OF YOURSELF

Turns out, treating ourselves is not the same thing as taking care of ourselves. Treats are pleasurable activities we do on occasion for a little bit of escape. They usually occur outside our homes. Examples include the occasional manicure or pedicure, haircut, night out with the girls, weekend away, or shopping spree. It may be a once-a-year vacation to our favorite place or a concert to see our favorite artist. When we treat ourselves, we feel momentary euphoria.

Treats are irregular and infrequent.

While they are enjoyable, they do not sustain our daily mental health. We are not happy all month because we have dinner out with the girls every six weeks. Treats are extras. They can take us from happy to happier, but they do not take us from depressed to content.

Treats are like dessert. Sweet and luxurious, but not the main meal. They are special and indulgent, but the ingredients aren't what our bodies need to stay healthy.

The day-to-day acts of taking care of ourselves, on the other hand, are like breakfast, lunch, or dinner. We need them to stay alive and healthy, and to have the energy to do what we need to do. Unlike treating ourselves, taking care of ourselves can happen every single day within our own homes.

> We need to take care of ourselves to stay alive and healthy, and to have the energy to do what we need to do.

No escape needed.

But before we get into specific ways you can take care of yourself daily, ask yourself this important question:

> *Do I think of taking care of myself as an indulgence or a necessity?*

If you feel that caring for yourself well is somehow selfish, indulgent, or frivolous, then you likely won't do it. You'll sacrifice your hygiene, health, and moods for your family. Never mind that abandoning yourself will leave you mentally, emotionally, and spiritually unwell and thus unable to care for your family well.

You probably feel guilty even thinking about having the kids wait or occupy themselves while you do something for you. Maybe it even seems sinful. If you felt that taking care of yourself was morally wrong, then there's no way you'd do it. In fact, mothers who find deep purpose in their parental role would not prioritize themselves over their children, as though they were more important. Ain't gonna happen.

It may feel like an either-or to you. Either you prioritize your children's needs and wants, or you prioritize your own. If that's the way you look at it, of course you'll abandon yourself and feel perfectly justified doing so. You want to be a loving, nurturing mother who meets her children's needs, not one who ignores those needs.

Luckily, this is not an either-or. It's not a win-lose. We do not need to choose our children or ourselves. We can, as responsible adults, care for both ourselves and our children. Sure, it may not feel as luxurious or exclusive as a weekend at a spa, but it can be just as restorative.

Prioritize sleep

Sleep is a hot topic among moms. It is also, apparently, controversial. As a certified baby and toddler sleep consultant, I know this too well. Moms feel so strongly about sleep—how to get it and how much is needed—that they will fight about it over the internet with total strangers from the opposite side of the world. They will insult each other to defend their own perspectives, and both will cite scientific studies that claim the exact opposite thing.

How soon babies learn to sleep on their own, where babies sleep, whether or not to co-sleep, and if so, when to stop co-sleeping, are all hotly debated. Then there are the related issues of whether or not to swaddle or carry your baby all day, and when to introduce a pacifier . . . any one of these may lead to all-out war.

Usually underneath all that arguing, debate, and anger are exhausted mothers trying to do their very best. Scientists, doctors, and humans the world over can agree on one simple principle: People need sleep.

One way to take care of yourself in your daily life is to get enough sleep. It is not glamorous, it's not fun, and in fact it may mean you have less time for fun, but it's absolutely vital to having stable moods. You cannot sustain good physical, mental, emotional, or spiritual health if you are chronically sleep deprived.

A few months of sleep disruption due to bringing home a baby is one thing; years of sleep disruption is another. Sleep studies show that fewer than seven hours of sleep contributes to obesity, diabetes, and heart issues. It negatively affects immune response and increases inflammation.

Sleep is a major need, yet it's often something we fail to prioritize. You can, however, take some relatively simple but deliberate steps to create boundaries around sleep.

Turn off your device at least one hour before bed and plug it in outside the bedroom.

Create calming evening rituals that help you wind down. A warm bath, a favorite cup of tea, a plush robe, comfortable pajamas, soft sheets, books (not dark murder mysteries or self-help titles), and time with your spouse are all ways to help get ready to sleep.

Use calming sounds (low enough you can hear the little ones if they make noises) and an eye mask as sleep associations.

Nap when little ones nap. Don't do projects or housework; just lie down and sleep. If you have little ones who are starting to get up during naptime, lie down with them.

Avoid starting projects in the late evening hours or drinking caffeine just to help you stay up. Projects and another cup of coffee can wait. Sleep cannot. And while there is that funny saying, "You can sleep when you're dead," the truth is that lack of sleep is associated with increased mortality.[1] So . . . there's that.

Care about your body and hygiene

I have a confession to make. My hair is red and super thick, so during my most stressful and hands-on season of motherhood, I would go two weeks without washing it. It never got that oily, and I just didn't care. I didn't care what I wore either since I felt fat in my clothes. What was the point in being choosy about what I put on in the morning?

I didn't wear makeup, I didn't wash my face, and I didn't moisturize, tone, or wax. I barely shaved. I felt haggard, harassed, and hostile. I didn't take any time to myself all day, and when my kids were in bed, I'd jump on the computer and try to get work done. I felt completely disconnected from my body and disliked my appearance so much that I just ignored it completely.

Instead of taking care of the body God had given me and celebrating how it had created and then sustained life, I resented the extra fat and cellulite in my midsection and the "fine lines" that started appearing on my face.

After ignoring myself for a while, the pendulum would swing, and I'd become obsessed with my body. I would exercise to punish myself for the extra pounds. I didn't choose exercises I liked or simply take joy in moving around or playing with the kids. I'd set unrealistic, overly optimistic fitness goals that I couldn't keep for two weeks. Then I'd berate myself for not following through.

When I was standing around, I'd find myself absently grabbing my love handles. Like old friends, I guess, I just wanted to check in. Were they smaller or larger? My husband would catch me and tell me I was beautiful. I'd feel embarrassed and hate my body even more.

Now I have multiple scars from a mastectomy and three follow-up surgeries, and at forty, I have more wrinkles than ever. I'm at a very healthy weight, but my love handles are still hanging around loyally. I have so many freckles that they all sort of connect into a weird semi-tan. And yet . . . I feel good about myself.

Why?

Because for the past few years I have learned to take care of myself daily. And we are always happier with the things we take care of. Consider adopting one or more of the simple self-care practices that follow:

Find a simple skin care routine you can do every morning or evening, or both.

Put on a little makeup, just for yourself. Maybe you stop with tinted moisturizer and mascara, or maybe you do much more. A few small touches will help you feel special.

Move your body regularly. If you hate the idea of joining a gym, take your family on regular walks. Stretch in the living room, get a mini trampoline to improve your lymphatic flow, or do simple weights while watching TV. Exercise releases endorphins, and it feels good to move.

Find some go-to healthy foods that you actually enjoy eating. Don't focus on depriving yourself, but concentrate on adding in good nutritious foods that increase your energy.

Get rid of clothes that don't fit. Replace them with clothes that do. Staring at a closet full of clothes you can't wear is bad for your self-esteem. If you want to get back into them one day, store them somewhere out of sight for now. Or better yet, commit to buying yourself a new wardrobe one day if you need it.

Choose clothing that is appropriate for your season of life. If you find yourself in workout gear at home and decide to change, don't reach for your college T-shirt first. Gather a small capsule wardrobe of appropriate daily wear and be more thoughtful about what you put on, even if the only people who see it aren't even potty-trained yet.

Fill a pampering basket with items you can use regularly. These might include Epsom salts, essential oils, and bubbles for warm baths; sugar scrubs, scalp and face massagers, and nice shampoos and conditioners for the shower; as well as lotions, spritzers, toners, and masks. It's not vanity to take care of the body God has given you.

Escape daily

A while ago, I was having coffee with Cypress, a pastor's wife in town who works with me on my website, A Mother Far from Home. She is calm, collected, and fully present in the moment. You can tell she's not obsessing about what she needs to do after our visit. She doesn't spend time telling me how she's failed at this or messed up at that. She is okay with herself. So much so that initially I found it unnerving.

How is she so calm? She does not appear to have gone into fight-or-flight one time in our hour-long visit. A miracle! And then I learned one of her secrets.

I was drinking coffee and eating my chocolate croissant while telling her the topic of this book. I said, "I hope moms can learn that it's okay to live within their own limits and boundaries and care for themselves well. You know . . . so they don't want to escape their own lives."

She smiled and said, "Oh, I escape my life every day."

It was like the coffee shop went quiet. My eyes locked on hers, and I said, "Tell me more."

"I escape in my own home. I go into my room and close the door, and the kids know to give me space for a while."

I set down my coffee cup and just stared at her in amazement. True, her kids are early elementary aged, not toddlers, so they are more independent. But without any shame, guilt, or personal condemnation, she'd taught them to give her time and space. Like it was the most natural thing in the world.

She escaped daily. In her own home. Not *from* her life but into a comfortable, calming place where she could be refreshed and replenished. It was so logical and rational that it almost seemed outlandish. Of course, if you have a baby and a toddler, it isn't quite as simple, but there are ways to take breaks. To escape into small, daily comforts—instead of living outside your limits and needs until you are mentally, emotionally, physically, and spiritually unwell and want to run away.

I realized I was experienced at abandoning my own needs and ignoring my own limits. I would burn the candle at both ends for a while, then flip out and call my mom to come get her grandkids and tell my husband I was running away from home. *Go with God. Best of luck. See you when I see you.*

Luckily, I'd generally broken that cycle. But my friend helped me see that this desire to escape—to get away from the weight of responsibilities and problems—was actually normal. And, in fact, we can indulge that feeling of escape daily. In healthy ways. Without abandoning our responsibilities or having to organize babysitting and a whole weekend away.

Make time for small, daily comforts

Look for small ways to refresh and reenergize yourself each day. I like to take a favorite drink and pretty blanket to our backyard where I can enjoy our country view and read a book. These small details make me feel physically comfortable and pampered, which helps me relax and recharge.

By finding small, normal ways to care for yourself during the day, you will regularly "fill your cup." If you make "escaping into your life" a normal practice, the cup doesn't stand a chance at remaining empty.

> Look for small ways to refresh and reenergize yourself each day.

Identifying and including these small, life-giving pleasures into your day may require a little bit of thought, likely some purchases, and maybe some organization, but they will make a huge difference in how much you enjoy life in your own home. It may seem overwhelming, but if you neglect self-care to the point that you constantly want to escape your own home, you are already in a bad spot. Here are some ideas on how you might find refreshment at home:

Keep your favorite drink on hand, get a special mug/glass, and create a comfy seating area. When you feel stressed or overwhelmed during the day, make a cup of your favorite drink and sit down—without your phone—to relax. Savor the drink and enjoy the comfortable seat. Put a soft blanket over you and rest until you feel refreshed.

Slow down as you do all the repetitive homemaking tasks. Instead of rushing through them, concentrate on what you're doing and do it well. Soon you'll find that your chores aren't stressful; they may even be calming. As you focus on what you're doing, you may land on some creative ideas, such as how to declutter an area that isn't working or something to purchase that will make life easier.

Don't let your kids (toddler and up) wake up at 4:30 a.m. and come out of their rooms just because they feel like it. Choose an appropriate and reasonable time each morning based on your child's sleep needs, and set your children's alarm clocks to that time. If they wake before it goes off, they can learn to play in their crib or their room until they hear the alarm. This will help you wake up each morning in peace and calm, not to screaming, crying, or banging. Before you jump out of bed, choose to spend a few quiet minutes in prayer, gathering your thoughts, or doing deep breathing—particularly if you already feel stressed at the thought of another long day.

Sit down with your meals and snacks and enjoy them. Don't scroll, read, or watch TV while eating. Enjoy the food you have prepared without rushing. You'll likely find you eat more nutritious foods in healthier quantities when you create these habits.

If you like to read, make time for it. You can read while your little ones nap or play. They don't need your undivided attention 24-7. Let them play while you read a chapter of a book.

Have a designated "escape" place in your home where you can go when your emotions get too high. Maybe it's your closet, an outside porch, or the bathroom. Put some encouraging devotionals there, and when the need to escape comes over you, go into that place to calm down.

Make sure your furniture is comfortable and you take time just to sit. Get some comfortable pillows and blankets. Your house doesn't have to be perfectly clean with everything done on your to-do list before you can sit.

You may like some of these ideas or come up with others. Every mama is different, but I encourage you to find ways to make your home a place of escape from the world. Make it comfortable and calming. If certain rooms stress you out, do what you can to change them now. If there's too much junk everywhere and nowhere to relax, declutter.

Your kids have one childhood, and you have one life. Don't waste them wishing you were somewhere else every day.

🔍 DISCOVER YOUR BOUNDARY MARKERS

1. Fill in the blank: "I am at my best when I get _____ hours of sleep."

2. If you do not get as much sleep as you need each night, list all the reasons why.

3. Do you take care of yourself well? If not, why not?

4. Does the idea of escaping in your own home each day make you feel lighter or heavier? Write out your thoughts.

⚑ PUT A FLAG ON THEM!

1. When I take care of myself by _____
_____, I feel more at peace.

2. I believe it [circle one] is / is not selfish to prioritize my
needs as I would prioritize the needs of my children.

3. I have abandoned the following practices since becoming
a mother:

4. I want to take the following self-care activities back:

▥ STRUCTURES, RULES, OR ROUTINES TO PROTECT YOUR BOUNDARIES

1. _____ is a great area I
could make into a mini escape zone within my own home.

2. When I begin to feel overwhelmed or the urge to escape
comes over me, I will do one of the following things to
help myself feel taken care of:

3. Here are some different rules or routines I can create and enforce with the kids to make sure both their needs and my own are met on a daily basis:

4. Take another look at your responses to question 2 under "Discover Your Boundary Markers." Jot down a possible solution for each one.

Example

Problem: To unwind before bedtime, I scroll through Instagram and fall asleep on the couch.

Solution: Put my phone "to bed" in another room and unwind with a novel.

CHAPTER 10

Minding Your Own Responsibilities

My FAMILY LIVES in the Florida Panhandle, not far from some of the world's most beautiful beaches, and we visit them a lot. I was raised on the sand and in the Gulf of Mexico, and I am raising my kids with the same love for salt water and the relaxing sound of waves.

Not long ago we took our five kids to the beach and started throwing a Frisbee together in a large circle. Some of the older kids got the hang of tossing and catching it pretty quickly, but my son, a kindergartner, was having a hard time mastering it. Which makes sense—catching a thin Frisbee coming at you quickly can be tricky.

It was his turn to catch the Frisbee, so he turned and faced my husband. As the plastic disk floated toward him, he reached out his hands to grab it. Instead of catching it cleanly or missing it entirely, the Frisbee smacked him hard on the wrist.

Even for an adult, this doesn't feel great, so I was getting ready to say something comforting or ask if he was okay when he looked directly at his dad and started in on him. "You threw the Frisbee and hurt me on purpose! You hurt me!"

Clearly, my son's wrist was hurt because he missed catching the Frisbee, not because my husband meant to hurt him, but to this child's mind, it had been purposeful. At first, I'll admit, this blame shifting and drama annoyed me and started killing the vibe. Then I realized that, actually, I do this too.

THE BLAME GAME

I used to subconsciously blame the kids or my husband for everything. I didn't even know I was doing it. I had decided to have the kids—they didn't choose to be born—and here I was blaming my problems on them.

Surprisingly, going from being an only child to living in a home with seven people, five of whom are little kids, has had its bumps. I'd feel resentful if they were noisy or annoyed if they got up and down from the table.

Never mind that I am loud, we had no noise rules, and the table wasn't completely set so they had to get up for drinks and silverware . . . it all felt like they were ganging up to irritate me. During a talk with a parenting mentor of mine, the topic of controlling our environment was mentioned. A light bulb went off! If I wanted my environment to be peaceful, then it was my responsibility to order that environment well.

It wasn't until I saw that I could let my annoyances lead me to better rules and routines—ones I was in charge of—that I started finding relief. I, the adult, could set us all up for success in both small and large ways.

I didn't like how something happened? I could change it. Not only was this great for me, but it was great for the kids. Who wants a mama who's always annoyed?

When I am in pain or things have gone sideways, I often look for quick relief by blaming someone else. It is, I like to say, mood-altering. When my keys aren't hanging by the door, I find myself saying, "Who lost my keys?"

It is I. I lost my keys.

Maybe you can relate. You stay up past midnight binge-watching a show, and then when the baby wakes at 2 a.m. for a feeding, you blame her for your exhaustion.

You've offered no toy organization system or chore expectations to your kids, and you blame them for leaving the house a mess.

You leave your phone ringer on and get mad when it rings. Then you answer it and get mad at the robot trying to sell you something.

You don't exercise or eat vegetables and then blame your genetics and thyroid for the weight gain.

You buy things you don't need and spend more than you earn, and yet you blame your boss for your money problems.

And on and on. It is hard when things don't go our way. We are already stressed and worried and then we think, *Another thing. Surely there must be some other person who can swoop in and act right and make my life easier.* I am the first to think, *Please, someone, rescue me!*

Sometimes, of course, other people actually mistreat us, causing us pain, hardship, and problems. And other times we're just at the wrong place at the wrong time. Or a tragic illness is out of our control. Some situations are so dire that only God can move and help us. Sometimes He intervenes in miraculous ways. Other times, He does not.

> Oh, how great are God's riches and wisdom and knowledge! How impossible it is for us to understand his decisions and his ways! For who can know the LORD's thoughts? Who knows enough to give him advice?
>
> Romans 11:33-34, NLT

Unfortunately, even when we are in deep as a result of unfortunate circumstances or others' bad choices, we still must act if there is action to take. At first this seems scary, but after a while, this knowledge brings great relief.

Blaming others feels immediately satisfying, taking some of the heat off ourselves and the burden from our shoulders. The trouble comes when we live in this constant state of blaming others. Living in this victim/rescuer paradigm makes life harder for us. If we see ourselves as victims of life, we are stuck waiting around for someone to rescue us. This mindset leaves us feeling powerless and out of control. And when we feel powerless and out of control, we end up anxious and stressed. And when we mamas are anxious and stressed, the kids are anxious and stressed.

OWN IT

If you want a happy and peaceful family life, you have to recognize your role in the home. A mother's role is both nurturer and leader. You are one of the adults—you may be the only adult—who gets to make and enforce the rules, set boundaries, and organize the flow of family life.

If the mornings are nuts, the afternoons are crazy, and the evenings are chaos, there's no point in blaming the children whose brains aren't fully formed yet. Yes, they may be making choices you don't like and doing things that make no sense to your adult brain, but that's because they aren't adults.

Luckily, you are. This is a responsibility, but it's also a privilege. And when you realize that not only can you make rules for everyone's safety but also for everyone's well-being—including your own—you'll start to feel excited and ready to take on your day.

The Bible calls you and me to do things in good order and to live lives that display the fruits of the Spirit: love, joy, peace, patience, kindness, goodness, faithfulness, gentleness, and self-control (Galatians 5:22-23). Whew, no small order. To accomplish this, you have to realize your own part in making sure both your life and your children's lives are peaceful.

Let's talk about things that are our own responsibility. This exercise shouldn't make you feel like you have more work to do; instead, it should help you see that you are actually fully equipped to make meaningful changes in areas that will bring you and your family more peace.

Your family routines

If the kids are up too early, stay up too late, and never help out around the house, it's time to change that. You are in charge of the family routines. You can buy clocks for the little kids' rooms so they know when it's time to start the day. You can create chore times and require everyone's participation.

You can have routines before and after dinner that involve everyone so you aren't the only one prepping dinner and cleaning the kitchen. You can have set bedtimes and create wind-down routines so everyone gets enough sleep, which also will improve their moods.

Family traditions, rituals, and daily habits will all be kept by you, the adult. The parts of the day that don't work can be changed. You can create routines so you aren't always running around like a chicken with its head cut off.

Once I had resigned as homeschool mom and enrolled my kids in the local schools, I knew the mornings could have been a time of insanity. If I wanted to get the kids to school without needing a daily massage from the stress, we needed a rock-solid routine. In the mornings, all the kids get up, get dressed, come downstairs, make their own break-fasts, get their backpacks, and are ready to go. I do very little in the mornings but put out occasional fires or comb some flyaway hairs.

If you'd like a reset, check out the three-day Family Routines Reboot at *amotherfarfromhome.com /routines-reboot.*

Establishing such routines may seem like a lot of work, but trust me, if you start with the parts of the day that are chaotic and turn those around, you'll be energized to create sustainable family routines.

Your schedule

No matter how full or unwieldy your schedule is, you are in charge of it. That's great news. The bad news is that if you have a lot of commitments, extracurriculars, and activities outside the home that you cannot handle, you may have to disappoint some people. And those people may be your kids.

If you can barely function, much less thrive, with practices five nights a week, music lessons once a week, work commitments some weekends, etc., then the answer is not to push through until you are exhausted from all the stress. The answer is to be honest with yourself, acknowledge your limits and boundaries, and pare down your schedule.

This may be a great time for your kids to get resourceful about how they can do the things they want to do without depending on you to be their chauffeur. If you have to leave some commitments or outside projects for your own sanity, then do so. It's better to be honest about your capacity than to overpromise and underdeliver.

One of my best friends changed jobs and took a large pay cut just to work better hours. It was a hard choice, but then it became the absolute best choice. Time is a limited resource, and once spent, you can never get it back.

Women who are overcommitted, overburdened, and miserable are not more noble or more spiritual. Do not commit to that which makes you nuts. It's not easy, but it's simple.

Your spiritual health

When life gets busy, our spiritual disciplines seem to be one of the first things to go. They don't seem quite as urgent or necessary as the other, more practical parts of life. However, when we neglect our spiritual lives, we end up feeling cut off from our life source. Instead of orienting ourselves to receive strength and peace from God, we end up running ourselves ragged in our own strength.

There are so many ways to strengthen ourselves spiritually now. Working through a daily devotional, praying, reading and meditating on Scripture, listening to podcasts, engaging with small groups or mom groups with childcare, and spending time with fellow believers—any of these habits will go a long way in keeping our eyes fixed on the eternal, not just on our current struggles. One benefit of our smartphones is easy access to great content. If you want spiritual resources that are available anywhere and anytime, check out apps like

YouVersion and Refresh: Daily Bible Devotionals. A strong spiritual life offers us strength, perspective, and wisdom, which directly translates into a calmer, more centered life.

Your mental health

Adult life is hard. Taking care of kids and the house and trying to stay married or get remarried; remaining in an active relationship with God; having a meaningful job or career; saving money for the future; and dealing with your own emotions, responsibilities, and current events—all of this is a lot.

In chapter 3, I mentioned what I learned about boundaries and limits from biking into the wind on Saint George Island. When things get hard and you are always riding straight into a strong wind, when you live beyond your spiritual, physical, emotional, and mental limits and boundaries, you suffer. And, unfortunately, no one shows up to save you from these feelings. You and I are the ones who must take care of ourselves so that we are okay.

I lived in Italy for nearly two years right after college and became fluent in Italian during that time. When you ask someone in Italian "How are you?" the phrase literally translates, "How do you stay?" And the answer, "I'm well" is translated, "I stay well." So I ask you, mama, are you staying well?

If not, why not?

No matter your situation, you always have options. In fact, the worse your mental state or practical circumstances are, the more important it is for you to exercise your own choices. No one but you is going to make sure you are at peace. You are the one who has to say, "Enough is enough."

> Get all the advice and instruction you can, so you will be wise the rest of your life.
>
> Proverbs 19:20, NLT

And the idea that you must grin and bear it for the rest of your life is both demoralizing and just not true.

There are always options, always choices, always ways out of the current situation. Organizing your life so that it doesn't make you crazy is not a luxury—it's a responsibility. And if you are so beat down that you cannot think straight, then you can find someone to help you do some problem-solving.

Your physical health

At times, the very hardest things to do are the best for you. But then, interestingly enough, when you turn the corner with the wind at your back, pushing you forward, you find that the best practices for your health are actually pleasant and addictive. They just plain ole make you feel better.

When I was diagnosed with cancer and began diving into research on full-body health, I was shocked at how unhealthy my habits were. I purposefully stuffed down my emotions, had erratic eating patterns, and avoided physical activity but then exercised to punish myself, just to name a few. I thought I was healthy enough BC, but as Chris Wark says, a cancer diagnosis has a way of tapping you on the shoulder, saying,

"The way you are living is killing you."[1] If I wanted to live, I had to make some changes.

While each of our bodies has slightly different needs depending on what we are going through, we all need healthy food, movement, and rest. Mothers everywhere don't sleep when they're tired. They don't rest when they're worn out. They don't eat when they're hungry (but they binge when they're emotional).

We are so good at putting our kids' physical needs in front of our own and then forgetting about our needs altogether. It's no wonder we suffer from weariness, burnout, and exhaustion at unprecedented rates. But the truth is that we can take care of ourselves *while* we take care of our kids. We don't have to choose between being a good mom and taking good care of ourselves.

Your stress level

You will be given as much load, work, and stress as you allow yourself to take on. Years ago my mom told me that when she left her job at the local power company to become an elementary teacher, it took three people to fill her roles. Without realizing it, she'd gradually begun doing the jobs of three people!

When you are capable, people ask you to help. When you work for yourself, there's always more to do. If you are a never-ending to-do-list maker, then the to-do list just gets longer and longer and more varied by topic.

When you've reached your mental, emotional, physical, and spiritual limits, no one will be there to make sure you stop. The person who has to mind your limits is you. Sometimes, unfortunately, drastic measures are necessary so you aren't living in a constant state of stress.

Are financial pressures too much? Some radical changes may be in order. Too much debt and your stomach is in knots from it all? As Dave Ramsey might say, sell it all off and downgrade. Get an older car and a smaller home; pay off the debt; and get out from under the crushing burden.

Does someone in the home have a job that is too stressful? It's time to stop blaming the boss, even if the boss is the one causing the stressful environment. Ask for what you want, stop doing unreasonable things, or quit. A small pay cut may be a worthwhile trade-off for not being miserable any longer.

Or maybe (no one wants to tell you this, so don't send me hate mail), maybe your own dreams are making you stressed. Every time you scroll Instagram, Facebook, or whatever new app is up by the time this book releases, you are exposed to people talking on and on about how they are hustling for their dreams, working eighteen-hour days to make money while they sleep.

Maybe staying up until 2 a.m. before getting back up at 5 a.m. to work on a dream that's costing you a lot of money and causing you a lot of stress isn't the ideal way to pass the one life you have with your kids. It may be worth it for a season, but if that season turns into your life, something's gotta give.

Your time

I wrote a blog post about why we never have enough time that got a huge response from moms.[2] One reason is that when the kids are really young, you and I tend to separate our days into two segments.

The first part is the hours when your kids are awake, and you feel you can do nothing but watch them, feed them, play with them, change diapers, and tend to their every need. The second comes when the kids are asleep. You are also asleep during a lot of these hours, but after you subtract those, you are left with a few short hours per day to get things done. Into that short window you try to fit all chores, administrative adult things, special projects, me time, side hustles, future planning, and anything else that requires concentration.

Trying to cram so much into that second part may be necessary for a short while, but ultimately it will drive you crazy. You may begin to resent the kids because you cannot get anything done during their waking hours and have so much to do that you can't fit it all into the hours they are asleep. One answer? As kids age, begin to involve them in as many of your tasks as you can. You won't be able to do that with everything, of course, but as you work on your adult responsibilities, the kids will learn patience and maybe even a few life skills along the way.

Another major reason mothers don't seem to have enough time is that you and I throw so much of it into the black hole we hold in our hand. We all know that our phones are

Through my digital detox journal, *Slow Your Scroll*, I help mothers break out of this time-sucking habit. See https://shop.amotherfarfromhome .com/products/slow-your-scroll.

addicting and convenient, and they are a great way to escape our momentary feelings of stress.

We all have the same 168 hours each week, so if you find yourself feeling stressed and beyond your limits primarily because you feel you don't have any time, sit down and start tracking how you use it for a week or two. You may be surprised to discover where your time seems to go and how you can take some of it back.

WAIT! THERE'S MORE

There are, of course, many areas of life that are your responsibility. If this makes you feel burdened or even angry, you are trying to ride into the wind and it is all too much right now. But there are likely many areas of life in which you can, with some thought, prayer, and intention, stop going against your limits and boundaries.

The key to living a life of wisdom, according to Psalm 90, is to realize how short life is. When you recognize that you have a limited number of days, weekends, vacations, movie nights, or lazy Saturdays with your family, you won't willingly waste them. No one is going to show up at your house and help you be the leader in your own life.

You've got to do it.

Once you realize that you can craft a life that is a blessing to you and those around you, you will start to see the things driving you crazy as flags indicating where your boundaries are being crossed. Next you can begin investigating these flags and start solving problems, because you realize that these problems are your responsibility. Even if these problems originate from someone else's foolish choices or bad behavior, what you're going to do about it is your problem now.

As you chip away at these trouble spots and become the leader and decision-maker of your own life, you can start riding with the wind behind you. The same path that used to be such hard work to navigate now

> Teach us to realize the brevity of life, so that we may grow in wisdom.
>
> Psalms 90:12, NLT

becomes easier. The dread and doom you used to feel every evening is now a more sporadic visitor. You start to see patterns and situations in your life where you have been waiting on an imaginary hero to show up and rescue you.

And then, guided by knowledge and the wisdom of the Lord, you can begin to act like someone who is balancing that bike. You are the one who can steer away from potholes and go down easier paths. You can recognize your boundary lines and work to stay within them.

Sure, you can't do it on your own, and you'll never do it all perfectly. But there is no one else who can do it for you, so you may as well get on with it.

🔍 DISCOVER YOUR BOUNDARY MARKERS

1. I am always waiting for someone or something to rescue me in situations like

2. I find myself regularly blaming other people for

3. When I think of taking responsibility for all of the areas of my life, it makes me feel very

🚩 PUT A FLAG ON THEM!

1. _____ is an area of my life in which I've put off taking ownership or avoided finding solutions for problems.

2. Instead of waiting to be rescued when I am feeling _____, I am going to start _____ _____.

3. I am responsible for _____,
and I can manage it how I see fit.

▦ STRUCTURES, RULES, OR ROUTINES TO PROTECT YOUR BOUNDARIES

1. The _____ part of our daily life feels chaotic.
I can put the following routines into place to make it more
peaceful:

2. Brainstorm some family rules that will help "control the
environment" of your home to make it more manageable
and peaceful for all.

3. What are some ways or new routines that will set up you
and your family for success?

CHAPTER 11

Minding Your Own Home

My husband and I had a lot of fights in our newlywed days. I was an only child with a strong personality and unrealistic ideas about marriage. He was extremely laid-back with equally unrealistic but opposite ideas about marriage. It made for a lot of lively discussions.

We were blessed with our firstborn daughter before we'd been married two years and our first son just over twelve months later. So from the beginning we were busy. Living in Australia without family nearby, I felt the weight of the world on my shoulders as I tried to organize our home life well. There was laundry, cleaning, cooking, decorating on a penny, and my new work-from-home job. So much to be done in a day.

And what is one of the things my husband likes best? Relaxing. It drove me insane. After we had put the little ones down to sleep for the night, I'd start my tidying habits or DIY projects aimed at making our tiny townhouse feel more like a home.

He'd sit on the couch and call me over to sit. I'd be walking from the laundry room to the kitchen, and he would pull me down to cuddle or chat. But instead of falling into the arms of the man who loved me, I would get so mad.

Didn't he see how the house was a mess?

Didn't he know how tired I was and how I wouldn't sleep well if I went to bed with all that needed doing left undone?

How could he just sit on the couch and stare out at a messy living room and a kitchen with a sink full of dirty dishes?

Was he missing part of his brain?

Now, after twelve years of marriage, I can confidently say this: He *is* missing part of his brain. The part that lets a little mess here or there rob him of his peace. His moods do not ebb and flow with the state of the house like mine do, which is good for him. But as a woman, mother, and homemaker, I still need my home to be peaceful and in order. It's just how I am. It's probably how you are too.

These days, after having adjusted my unrealistic expectations, I have learned to see life as a video, not a photograph, and I've accepted that my worth or lovability does not come from my performance. I am also less frantic about my home.

I no longer view piles of toys or dust as a sign that I am a lazy, undisciplined person, but as a sign that people live here. When I see cobwebs in a bathroom corner, I no longer burst into tears and then ugly-cry for fifteen minutes. Been there, done that. Zero stars. *Do not recommend.*

I no longer view piles of toys or dust as a sign that I am lazy or undisciplined, but as a sign that people live here.

Still, I don't want a chaotic, messy house. I want my home to be a place of comfort, peace, and safety for me and my family. A haven from outside life. I want to walk from the minivan to the back door and enter my home breathing a sigh of relief. I want my home to be a place that is lovely to me. Not because it's on trend or has the latest gadgets, but because I feel at peace there.

Don't you?

HOW DOES YOUR HOME AFFECT YOU?

Right now, without overthinking it, what words come to mind to describe the state of your home? Is it peaceful and welcoming or messy and stressful? There is no right or wrong answer here; the key is to discover how you feel about your home environment.

This is important, mama, because when your home is a place of stress, your subconscious mind will keep coming up with ways to escape it. And the more you find ways to escape having to deal with your home environment, the worse it gets. It's what I call an unhappy cycle that leads to distress and survival mode.

Imagine this for a minute . . .

You've had a lovely day out with friends, and your heart is light. You drive home, park the car, grab your bag, and start the walk inside. You're in a happy mood as you get closer to the door. Then you open it, walk inside, and immediately you feel _____.

If you feel relieved, content, and at rest, congratulations. Your home environment gives you peace. This is the goal. After all, through the prophet Isaiah, we know what God wants for us: "My people will live in peaceful dwelling places, in secure homes, in undisturbed places of rest" (Isaiah 32:18, NIV).

If, on the other hand, the thought of walking into your home after a lovely day away makes you feel stressed, distressed, or depressed, then your home has room for improvement. Take heart, we'll get you there.

Your home can be a place of peace, and there's nobody better suited to make that happen than you, even if your family is less than enthusiastic and not quite on board yet. You may feel like your house is out of control, but with a few tweaks here and there, you can take back control and make the home peaceful for everyone.

GET RID OF STUFF FIRST

The word *organizing* has a nice feel to it. It suggests that life will be better when we alphabetize and arrange. When our closets are color coded, our pantry containers are labeled, and our Tupperware containers are matched, we will feel in control. These things can be extremely satisfying to do as one-off projects, but they rarely work long-term.

Why? They require a lot of upkeep. Micro-organizing—organizing in a very detailed manner—takes a lot of maintenance and isn't self-sustaining. If everyone in the home isn't on board with your system, you'll end up frustrated, and the whole thing will go to pot. You spent twenty-five dollars on a label maker, and look where it got you.

There's a better way. Instead of trying to organize all your stuff, get rid of a lot of stuff. This is easy for me to say because I love throwing things out. When I get stressed or overwhelmed, I grab some trash bags and go through the house finding things to throw out, donate, or give away.

It is an instant mood lifter for me.

But even if you have pack-rat tendencies like my husband, who will keep used batteries in case they might come in handy later, you will feel relief when you rid your home of things that do not serve any purpose.

In fact, when you keep only the things you use and need, you'll find there's very little to organize and much less to clean and keep tidy in your home. You don't need elaborate pot-and-pan storage systems when you just have a couple of

> When you keep only the things you use and need, you'll find there's very little to organize and much less to clean and keep tidy.

each. There's no need for kitchen drawer organizers when you only have a handful of utensils you use on a regular or semiregular basis.

Having lived in four countries outside the US—England, Scotland, Italy, and Australia—I can tell you this: Americans have a stuff problem. In 2021, more than 10 percent of American households rented storage units. These families pay around ninety dollars a month to keep all the items that won't fit in their homes.[1]

With the exception of Canada, homes in America are generally larger than those in the rest of the world too. So we have larger houses to fill with more stuff, and we still need storage units to hold all the extra stuff we keep because we might need it. We have this stuff, if we're honest, because we can't let go of it emotionally. Unfortunately, these belongings are now a line item on our budget and take up mental space because the storage unit is something else we have to manage.

If you think of environments you love to be in, you'll probably notice that most of them are not overcluttered and full of stuff. Simplifying makes life less stressful. Choose one area at a time and be merciless. Get rid of broken, old, or unused items. Donate, throw out, give to friends, or sell. Be mindful of your children's or husband's sentimental things, of course. If your home is like mine, I bring in most of the excess stuff anyway, so it's mine to clear out.

Don't overthink it. Sorting is very hard at first, but then it's like pushing a snowball downhill. The more you simplify, the more you enjoy it. The less filled up and overflowing your home is, the better you feel and the more motivated you are to continue.

No need to create these outlandish goals you won't keep. Just start small and celebrate quick wins. Think about it as a season of simplifying, not a gargantuan task you need to do in a month. Appreciate how good it feels to have less clutter in your home. Let the little successes motivate you to pursue larger ones.

GETTING EVERYONE ON BOARD

No chapter about our homes would be complete without mentioning that it's usually the little people who create the most messes. In fact, I think one-year-olds make the biggest ones. They walk from one room to the other and grab everything in arm's reach, only to drop it on the floor. Throw pillows, cups, decorative objects, toys—literally anything they can grab hold of, they will toss.

Messes get more concentrated as the kids get older. They start building extensive forts with every pillow and blanket in the house. They use their imagination to build creations that take up half the floor in their rooms. And that's not to mention their dirty clothes, unmade beds, snack bowls, and scattered toys.

Luckily, children are just as capable of cleaning up their messes as they are of making them. And if you need even more motivation to get your kids helping around the house, know this: Numerous studies now show that children who do chores growing up become more successful adults.

Marty Rossmann, a professor emeritus at the University of Minnesota, researched the benefits to children who are assigned household tasks from an early age. Kris Loubert with the Early Childhood Family Education program in Minneapolis schools comments on Rossmann's findings:

> I hear parents of young children complain about how difficult it is to get kids to cooperate and how difficult it is for them to follow through with their children to the completion of a task. They often will say it [is] easier if they just do the housework themselves. I believe Rossmann's findings could create more resolve in parents to teach, work with, and be more patient with their children as they learn how to contribute to the upkeep of the family home. Teach your kids responsibility and contribution at home early and they are likely to be successful later in life.[2]

HOW TO GET CHILDREN TO HELP

It feels heavy and hard to get kids to cooperate when they aren't used to it. If they're older, they may complain and talk back. If they are young, they often lack focus and don't do the job as well as we'd like. Other barriers to having our little ones help include the sense of pride we feel when we do it all ourselves, or the feeling that we are not very noble or godly if we don't take on all of the homemaking.

Moms who stay at home may see all of the domestic tasks as their job; they might believe that it isn't fair or right to delegate chores when they are home all day. But that isn't the point, is it? We ask kids to chip in and take part in running the house, not just to take weight off Mom, but simply to share the home responsibilities and to teach kids life skills and a work ethic.

Even if children have never helped in the kitchen or the main living areas (and they should), there are still plenty of chores to keep them busy in their own rooms and with their own self-care and hygiene.

Here are some general rules of thumb for having a home that is run by all those who live in it, not just mama.

Work before play

Before my husband and I were married, we went on a mission trip to South Africa, where a local pastor told us we needed to adapt to South African Time. By this, he meant, you simply do one thing before the next. It doesn't really matter what time something is supposed to happen. You do one thing, then the next, then the next. You don't jump ahead. You simply finish the first thing, then move on to the next.

Adopt this mindset at home. Before doing something pleasant, get chores out of the way. That way, the pleasant activity acts as a carrot to get the work done. This results in far less nagging, cajoling, and—eventually—yelling.

Little kids can't watch TV, play outside, or play with

friends until they've done their chores. Beds are made before they go outside. Rooms are cleaned before lunch. Chores come before screen time, going out with friends, or heading to practice or games. You get the idea. Ordering activities this way will result in a lot less resistance.

Playtime and outside activities are extras and privileges; they are not more important than personal responsibility. First comes an ordered personal home life; after that, kids' schedules can expand so they're responsible for extra commitments.

Chores aren't one-size-fits-all

If you are a mom who loves to plan and organize, some type of weekly chore rotation or chore chart may work well. You can figure out what needs to be done and by whom, then post a chore schedule in an easy-to-see place. This will help keep the kids accountable to their assigned chores.

If you are more "go with the flow," you may simply have everyone pitch in when everyone is home. You choose which tasks need doing, split them up, and have everyone help with them. This makes the work go by faster so a lot gets done in a short period of time. After dinner, for instance, everyone may chip in to load the dishwasher, sweep or vacuum, and clear the table.

As kids get older, you may assign them weekly chores and give them deadlines. If the chores aren't done by that designated time, they will face certain consequences, decided ahead of time. Home life comes before social life.

Paying kids for chores isn't shown to work

Ralph Waldo Emerson said, "The reward of a thing well done is having done it."

We are expected to do many things without any tangible reward. We simply do them because they need doing. If we begin paying our children for all the little chores, we end up in a scenario where we have to pay our kids to clean up their own messes. Then when there is no outside motivation for them to do a task, they simply won't.

You may have some specific paid jobs the kids can volunteer to do, but paying your child for things like making their beds or putting away the dishes will backfire. It short-circuits a child's ability to develop self-motivation. It also fosters a "What's in it for me?" attitude.

Require your kids to do chores because they live in your house. Get a clear idea of what your children's basic responsibilities and privileges are. Then if the responsibilities are not done, remove the privileges.

It may not be easy, but it's simple enough.

FOR MAMAS WHO HAVE NO HELP

What if you are a single mom or a military spouse with a husband who regularly deploys? What if you live far away from family or are married to a man who won't lift a finger? Whatever your situation, there may be times when there is no other adult to help you get everything done.

It may feel like the weight of the world is on your

shoulders. If this describes how you're feeling, take heart. You are doing the best you can, and God sees what's done in private. Hopefully you are able to find peace and joy deep within through prayer, meditation on Scripture, and support from friends. That's the first step, but it doesn't do the dishes.

The advice I give in all of these scenarios is essentially the same. You are both in charge of these things and the one getting them done. As a result, you need to make life as easy as possible on yourself. You can and should identify your own standards, limits, and boundaries and operate within those.

Let me give you an illustration. Years ago when we lived in Australia, my husband and I went to dinner at another family's home. They had three elementary-aged children at the time. The wife told us how her oldest was born very premature, so they spent months going back and forth to the hospital.

She said each pregnancy and postpartum period had its challenges. Then she said something I will never forget. In fact, I have shared it with countless others because it was so refreshing. During these difficult times—late pregnancy, postpartum, etc.—she announced to her family that the standard at dinnertime had changed.

The new goal for her dinners was this and only this: They were edible. If they tasted good, well, that was a bonus. I laughed when she told me this, as though she were joking. In a stone-cold, sober tone, she assured me she was serious. Her goal was to put something reasonably nutritious and as simple as possible on the table.

When she was already stressed to the max, she didn't surf for new recipes, try out new ingredients, or worry about plate presentation. These were desperate times. Food in the belly was good enough. After those seasons passed, she gradually began cooking more "normal" meals again. Because she could.

My friend had gotten hold of something that will serve many of us well today. The truth is this: We can and should make every aspect of our home lives as simple as possible *for us* if we are the ones having to do it all. If we are responsible for making sure it's done, we get to choose *how* it's done.

Here are a few examples of how this might play out, just to get the wheels turning in your head. Every mom has different areas that cause the most stress.

- Some moms use only paper plates to avoid all the hassle of washing. Of course, they're not as good for the environment, but environmental activism is way higher up on Maslow's Hierarchy of Needs. If you are at your wit's end, find relief where you can.

- Is laundry a nightmare that never ends? I have a friend who got rid of all but seven or so outfits per child. And none of the clothing needs ironing. Laundry once a week is a breeze, putting the clothes away is a breeze, and no one is spending hours folding and sorting.

- Toys all over the house that no one cleans up but you? Create a new rule (for those old enough to understand it) that toys left on the floor will be removed. Ruthlessly declutter toys that are broken, unused, or not played with. When there are only a few toys, there will never be a mess.

Those are just three small examples, but you can extend the basic principle to all your responsibilities. How can you fulfill each duty as simply as possible so you don't drive yourself into the ground? Brainstorm some ideas. Try out different solutions. You can make life easier on yourself.

If you find yourself the main caregiver, home administrator, and boo-boo kisser, do yourself a favor and ruthlessly simplify. When life is simple, you're less stressed and anxious. When you're less stressed and anxious, you are a happier mother. When you're a happy mom, life is better for everyone.

DISCOVER YOUR BOUNDARY MARKERS

1. I feel resentful when I notice _____

_____ in my home.

2. My children's attitude toward helping out is_____

_____, and that makes me feel

_____

_____.

3. I am responsible for ____ percent of the running of the home. That makes me feel _____

_____.

🚩 PUT A FLAG ON THEM!

1. I feel at peace when my home is _____
_____.

2. I feel ill at ease, stressed, and overwhelmed in my home when _____
_____ because _____
_____.

3. I want my home to feel _____
_____ for my family.

▦ STRUCTURES, RULES, OR ROUTINES TO PROTECT YOUR BOUNDARIES

1. Brainstorm tidying and cleaning routines for the kids:

2. Brainstorm tidying and cleaning routines for myself:

3. Brainstorm consequences for not contributing to home systems:

CHAPTER 12

Minding Your Own Life

MOTHERHOOD CAN MAKE US FEEL as if someone hit a pause button on our lives. Before kids, I lived in Europe, traveled the world, learned a few languages, did what I wanted, went where I wanted, and answered to no one but God and the bottom of my wallet.

I could stay up late and make up the sleep whenever I felt like it, exercise for two hours a day, make a meal just for myself, and not include anyone else's needs or wants into my decision-making processes. I was responsible for myself and, for the most part, was the only one affected by my daily decisions.

I kept short accounts with myself. If I was tired, I slept. If I was hungry, I ate. If I felt stressed, I went for a run. (Just kidding—for a walk.) If I was struggling or had a spiritual question, I met with friends or pastors, or I went to church. If I needed some girl time, I organized a coffee date or night out with friends without a second thought.

I was responsible for my life, and it was pretty easy to make good decisions. Then I got married and had kids. Our two or three sessions of premarital counseling did not prepare me for how hard managing my own mental, emotional, physical, and spiritual needs would be now that I had to take other people into account.

Talk about a shock to the system for an only child like myself.

When we have babies, we are responsive to their every need. We go from being fully independent to being completely responsive to and responsible for another human being. And because we are consumed with love for this child, it is something we're willing to do. Add more kids, and now our lives are so full of other people's needs, wants, and desires that we are often just running around putting out one fire after the other.

It can be utterly exhausting. For moms who are really struggling, it can feel as if there's no end in sight. No way to make life more enjoyable. These moms feel unhappy and think it's just something they have to live with.

As we near the end of the book, I want to challenge you once more to look at two tendencies that cause many women unnecessary stress. When we feel overwhelmed or disoriented, we go into survival mode and are inclined to (1) focus on the future to help get us through the present, or (2) try to regain a sense of control by taking on even more responsibilities.

Let's review these impulses one at a time. As we do, consider what changes you want to explore or implement now that you've considered how you mind your household rules, personal standards, friendships, emotions, self-care, responsibilities, and home life.

#1: WE TEND TO FOCUS ON THE FUTURE INSTEAD OF LIVE IN THE PRESENT

Have you ever heard that it's important to have something to look forward to? That having some exciting future plans will make our everyday humdrum life endurable while we wait for that future day to come? As I mentioned in chapter 2, I think our culture encourages us to idealize the future.

It's true that anticipation and expectation keep us moving forward. The promise of the future is a strong motivating carrot, and it's why we work toward goals in the first place. Interestingly, cancer patients who are feeling discouraged are often advised to follow this strategy. In dire circumstances, looking forward to some future date on a calendar can actually give you the will to live.

I saw this principle play out firsthand as my grandmother, whom I called Mema, was dying of natural causes a few months after her ninety-third birthday. I was getting chemotherapy at the same time. The final weeks of her life took place as my chemo was drawing to a close. I had my treatments every Friday afternoon for twelve weeks, and during my final week one of our family friends, who loved my grandmother very much, told me something profound: "I think she's hanging on to make sure you are okay."

Growing up, I was always close to my grandmother. We lived less than a mile apart on a country road, and I walked that road almost daily during the summers. I stayed with her countless days and nights. I swam in her pool. I recovered from chicken pox wearing the white satin gloves she bought at Goodwill to keep me from scratching. I had Sunday lunches after church with her and Papa more than at my own house, and we wrote letters to each other throughout my twenties. Once when I was making a particularly hard decision about what to do with my future, she gave me a timely word from her devotion, "Don't be afraid to go out on a limb. That's where the fruit is."[1]

As I thought about my sweet Mema, I decided there was something to my friend's observation. Late that Wednesday afternoon, I dragged my worn-out, chemo-laden body to Mema's house as she lay in her hospital bed. I took her hand in mine and told her how much I loved her and how God had used her to put me on the straight path. I told her I would be finishing treatment on Friday and that I truly believed I would be okay. No matter what my future held, I'd be okay. Then I released her from her grandmotherly duties.

Less than twenty-four hours after my last cancer treatment, she went to be with her Lord.

Clinging to a future date can give us the motivation and encouragement to keep going through hard times. But what happens when our entire life becomes a hard time? What happens when, instead of looking forward to coming events, we begin to dread each day and focus obsessively on how things will be in the future?

It's as if we think once the future shows up, our problems will be gone. This attitude can actually cause us to live lives we don't like, if we let it go unchecked. If we spend our days, weeks, months, and years waiting for what may never come, we train ourselves to be unhappy in the present.

Here are some common refrains going through weary moms' heads:

1. *I can't wait until the baby sleeps through the night.*
2. *It'll be nice when the baby is weaned so I can have more than a three-hour break.*
3. *When my little one goes to school, I'll have more free time.*
4. *When my business gets off the ground, life will be less stressful.* (Spoiler alert: No, it won't.)
5. *I'll be happier when my house is bigger, I'm back in my prepregnancy clothes, and I can take nice vacations.*

It isn't that reaching toward goals is bad, of course, but cultivating a habit of living for a future that we aren't

> Cultivating a habit of living for a future that we aren't guaranteed short-circuits our joy in the present.

guaranteed short-circuits our joy in the present. It also prevents us from problem-solving in the areas where we are struggling.

Many moms live for the day when their little ones will sleep through the night, not realizing that they could achieve this milestone with just a few habit and routine changes. They wait for the day their kids can go to school, rather than finding ways to have affordable childcare and babysitting now to allow them some free time.

Lots of moms wish for a bigger, better house. But rather than trying to find ways to make their current space work better, they obsess on their future house at the expense of their current one.

If we ignore the present to focus on the future, we end up with a present full of unsolved problems. We hope these issues will just disappear one day. In reality, the future probably will show up looking a lot like the present—snap!—and our problems will still be there, sometimes with compounded interest.

The solution?

Work on the areas of life you do not like and find solutions that help your family now. Then strive toward future goals while having peace in the present. You can enjoy your life with your family today while looking forward to some point in the future, but without waiting for the future to save you.

Remember, the future doesn't really even exist because when we get there, it's then the present. We only ever have the present and all our past moments, which were once our present moments.

The anticipation and joy of the future can be sweet motivators for us, but they shouldn't be our lifeline.

#2: MOMS TRY TO FIGHT THEIR INNER TURMOIL BY ADDING MORE

I believe the second common strategy used by mothers stems from feeling out of control. Moms are worn-out, weary, and discouraged, running around like chickens with their heads cut off and feeling like they have no say in what's happening in their own lives.

Moms may do everything for the kids and manage all the family's administrative tasks, the home, their spouse's calendar, and their own jobs, if they have them. No wonder they can feel completely overwhelmed with everything that must be done.

Then when life is full enough, someone gets an ear infection, the pipes burst, an unexpected bill comes due, and the internet goes out. When it seems like the logical choice would be to ruthlessly eliminate every single thing that can be eliminated, instead . . . we decide we will feel more in control if we add more responsibilities, so we can make sure we are in the driver's seat of our own lives.

Let me give an example.

Lindsay has three kids, ranging in age from twelve to one. The older kids are in clubs and after-school activities, and the baby is just snacking round the clock, napping, and destroying the house all day, every day.

Lindsay works part-time so she is at work some, at home some. She manages the groceries, the cooking, the budget, the schlepping to and fro, the morning routine, the school pickups and drop-offs, the planning for vacations and special family memory-making activities—you know, like corn mazes. She feels like life is out of control and she has lost her sense of identity. She barely remembers what she liked to do before having kids and struggles to make time for herself.

So what does she do?

She decides she needs to do something more exciting just for her. Makes sense. She feels as though she has abandoned herself, and in many ways, she has. She joins a gym and wakes up at 5 a.m. a few days a week to go work out.

Lindsay thinks life will be more flexible and less stressful if she is self-employed, so she researches work-from-home options and launches some new social media handles, trying to build a following.

Adding these activities helps her envision a future that is less stressful than the present, and she feels more in control because she is taking the reins on the parts of her life where she can. Since other parts of her life feel so out of control, she initially finds comfort in her decision to take on more.

So where does that leave Lindsay? Is her plan successful?

She still manages the groceries, the cooking, the budget, the schlepping to and fro, the morning routine, the school pickups and drop-offs, the planning for vacations and special family memory-making activities. Plus now she wakes up early to work out and goes to bed late so she can work to get her new business off the ground.

She's getting half the sleep and doing twice the work.

Her strategy to make life easier has made life harder.

Even the most capable mothers can wither under the weight of it all. In fact, it is the most capable moms who end up in this position most often. Why? Because they understand their God-given ability to juggle and are confident that they can get it all done. They know they are responsible and capable. They will ride into the wind all day long, trusting that by sheer force of will, they will arrive at their destination. Even if they're dirty, achy, and half dead.

And it all seems to work—until one day it doesn't. One day, when enough is enough, Mom cracks. The straw that breaks the camel's back, so to speak. Or as they say in Italy, the drop that overflows the bowl. The answer is rarely ever to add more to make life more stable.

IMAGINE YOUR LIFE AS A BRIDGE

Picture a long, elegant bridge that is starting to crack or become structurally compromised. It was built years ago for cars, and now heavy-laden semis use it all day every day. The answer isn't to allow increasingly heavy vehicles to keep using it. That'd be homicide.

Instead, you investigate the problem. You find the weaknesses that will lead to disaster, create a repair plan, determine actual limits based on what the bridge can withstand, repair the faults, and then enforce the new limits needed to keep everyone who uses that bridge safe. Or you tear the bridge down and build a whole new one.

Likewise, you and I need to focus on our inner lives first. You figure out what isn't working and start living within your own limits, creating rules and boundaries in your home that keep you well. Only then can you add good activities and relationships on top, when you are mentally, emotionally, and physically able to support them all. But not before.

This may mean you drop all extracurriculars, cook the same seven family dinners each week, stop homeschooling (or start homeschooling), sell your car with the too-high car payment and buy a car with cash, move to a new city or move back to an old city. You may have to make some drastic changes. So what?

You and I are experienced at doing drastic things. After having other adults manage our lives for eighteen-plus years, we move out and start taking care of ourselves. We decide to sign a contract before God to live with another person and deal with all their drama until we die. We grow babies inside of ourselves, and then after a few hours of feeling like we might die, we give birth and commit to taking care of and loving these babies, again until we die. If those things aren't drastic, I don't know what is.

Only you know what simplifying your life will look like for your family. Once you decide to really tackle the issues that are causing the family bridge to weaken, you'll be amazed at how many ideas come up. And even contemplating all these possibilities could bring a sense of power and control, which is what you needed in the first place.

ORDERING YOUR PRIVATE WORLD

What is causing you stress? How can you fix those things now? What contributes to your feeling overwhelmed by finances, schedule, and workload? Many mothers feel selfish even thinking about prioritizing their inner lives. They worry that spending too much time thinking through the sources of their angst is unproductive.

It is true that, if left unchecked, we can veer into navel-gazing and become obsessed with thinking about and talking about our problems. Often, though, navel-gazing is a habit we adopt because our brains keep bringing us back to real problems that need to be addressed.

It's your job to create a life you like living. It's not anyone else's responsibility. You may find love and support from family and friends, but they cannot make your life peaceful. If something about your life is bugging you, don't ignore it and beg God for deliverance. Instead, as much as you can, fix it so that it doesn't drive you nuts.

> Wisdom is shown to be right by the lives of those who follow it.
>
> Luke 7:35, NLT

Sometimes very simple solutions will make an immediate difference in the home—like hiring a cleaning service, assigning chores to kids, or coming up with a new storage solution. Look for ways to bring down your stress level, like resigning from committees, groups, or responsibilities that "would be nice" but actually make your life awful. This isn't forever; it's until you aren't on the verge of a daily breakdown. Other people will understand. If they don't, it may be because they are ignoring their own feelings of being overextended and can't believe you are trying to break free.

When you realize that many of the little things in life are within your control, you can begin to take charge of your life and make it more pleasant. There is no spiritual benefit to being miserable for the sake of being miserable. It is no great testimony to keep yourself in a state of stress, anxiety, and weariness when you could make wiser choices and live a life of peace.

It's amazing how you can begin to major on the majors and minor on the minors when your inner world is in order and peaceful. Instead of becoming more selfish, you become more generous. Instead of thinking only of yourself, you have the headspace, time, and compassion to think of and serve others.

When you have more capacity for life, God will bring you the people or situations that allow you to love others. You'll have time to do the types of things you always wanted to do but couldn't when you were busy running around like a puppy chasing its tail.

Soon, on your quest to make your own life more peaceful and less stressful, you will find yourself content. You'll realize that in many areas of life you quickly arrive at a place of diminishing returns. You might actually be happier in a larger house if your current one is too crowded, but a huge house won't make you much happier than a house that is just big enough.

When you feel as if you're on a ship headed underwater, you may assume that you're about to drown and that life is against you. All the things that aren't going well are right there in front of you. When you truly take hold of the fact that God is the creator and controller of the sea, the wind, and the weather, but you are the captain of your own ship, you will start being more deliberate with your vessel. From that place of peace, life isn't as frantic. Once the waters are calmer, you start seeing ways to fix some of those annoyances. Or you decide you just don't care about certain activities or possessions anymore and throw them overboard.

Prayerfully evaluate your life and make ruthless changes that bring you peace. Consider taking a different way to your destination instead of the route with the most wind resistance. Your family needs you at peace more than they need the latest gadget, practice, or vacation.

SOMETIMES WE ALREADY HAVE WHAT WE NEED

At times we are in dire need, and something's got to give. We need money to avoid foreclosure, a job to pay the bills, medical help for healing, or wise advice to get us out of a troubling situation. Obviously these are real struggles and real circumstances that need real interventions.

More often, however, we are simply overwhelmed by life's mundane but unrelenting demands. Add to that the fact that we live in a society obsessed with productivity, efficiency, goal-setting, and more, more, more. But as long as we are fixated on our circumstances or our future, we will be in a constant state of unhappiness, frustration, and anxiety. We can never be content if we refuse to see the many blessings that surround us today.

No wonder we often lose sight of the fact that we generally have what we need now. And that, in every situation, God will provide the essentials we lack.

That truth reminds me of the well-known story of the wealthy banker who met a local fisherman while vacationing in a small coastal village.[2] When the banker asked the local how long he spent fishing every day, the man explained that he worked just enough to provide for his family's needs. That left him plenty of time, he said, to sleep in, play with his kids, relax with his wife, and hang out with his friends.

The banker told the fisherman how rich he could become if he just spent more of his time on the boat. In fact, if the fisherman worked really hard to expand his fishing enterprise, the rich tourist said, he might even be able to retire a millionaire in a decade or two.

The fisherman looked confused. "Why would I want to do that?"

The banker said, "Why, then you'd have plenty of time to sleep in, play with your kids, relax with your wife, and hang out with your friends."

Gratitude is not privilege; it's a choice. As the fisherman knew, there are always things to be happy about right now, and God's Word commands us to give thanks in every circumstance (see 1 Thessalonians 5:18). That doesn't mean we need to pretend to be happy about things we aren't happy about but that we acknowledge the things we do love and are thankful for. Gratitude changes how we feel and how we live. It, like the rest of God's commands, is for our own good, not harm.

Gratitude also reminds us that we have all we need to enjoy life right now. Even if our circumstances aren't perfect. It's entirely possible that we are pushing ourselves too hard. We are trying to do more, do better, and improve our lives so we can enjoy people, places, and events later—when, actually, we could enjoy all those things right now. If we let ourselves.

🔍 DISCOVER YOUR BOUNDARY MARKERS

1. I tend to live for a time in the future, looking forward to when _____

   _____.

2. I will be happier when _____

   because it will mean _____

   _____.

3. It feels impossible to be satisfied with _____

   _____ right now because _____

   _____.

⚑ PUT A FLAG ON THEM!

1. My life gets more stressful and unwieldy when I

2. I [circle one] do / do not find myself adding more and
   more to my life in an effort to gain some control.

3. I feel most out of control in my life when

▦ STRUCTURES, RULES, OR ROUTINES TO PROTECT YOUR BOUNDARIES

1. In order to enjoy my current life more, I will stop

2. In order to enjoy my current life more, I will start

3. The story about the rich vacationer and the fisherman
   helps me see these blessings in my life right now:

CHAPTER 13

Your True North

WHEN I WAS WATCHING TV AS A CHILD, I had to stand up and walk over to the set to manually change the channel. I used a typewriter in my room to type important things like *The Fresh Prince of Bel-Air*'s theme song. I recorded mixtapes from the radio, and Mariah Carey's *Hero* was my first CD. My first cell phone didn't have caller ID. I had to attend all my college classes in person. Before driving somewhere for the first time, I printed out directions from MapQuest, and if I got lost, well, I stopped and asked for directions.

Now I can watch TV, find directions, take classes, listen to music, order groceries, and track my period, my ovulation, and my stocks from a tiny computer I keep in my purse.

A lot can change in a few decades.

Some things, though, don't really change. The majors are still majors, even if they look different. The God of yesterday, today, and tomorrow never changes. His commandments for right living are still wise and produce good fruit. A loving, stable family life helps children grow up securely attached and resilient. A happy mom raises happier kids. And burning the candle at both ends makes everyone miserable.

All these things were true then and are true now.

We didn't look forward to adulthood just to wake up day after day, biking straight into heavy winds that leave us exhausted and discouraged. Wasn't adulthood supposed to be fun? Didn't it mean we would be our own boss and get to do whatever we wanted?

A while ago, on a particularly stressful day, I had an epiphany about my own kids.

My husband and I have worked hard to be sure they are well-loved, well-fed, and well-clothed and have plenty of opportunity for fun and excitement. In their short lives, they have seen a lot of places and done a lot of things. I thought about how fun childhood is for them, how full of curiosities and adventure. They have swum with dolphins, snorkeled in the Caribbean, spent summers on the beautiful beaches of the Gulf of Mexico, learned the banjo, keyboard, and guitar, played sports, adventured through our woods, flown on planes, ridden on boats, and just generally had fantastic lives.

And then I thought about adulthood. Was I running myself into the ground becoming a miserable adult so my children could have an amazing childhood? If I asked them to tell me what it means to be an adult based on what they'd seen in me, would they say it involved being stressed and strung out?

> Was I running myself into the ground becoming a miserable adult so my children could have an amazing childhood?

It made me think, *If my kids get all the fun of childhood and no taste of responsibility, will they want to grow into adults doing all the responsible work and having none of the fun?*

If this is happening all over, it's no wonder kids seem more immature and entitled than ever before. I didn't want my own life to be a cautionary tale. I decided then and there to make adulthood something my kids will look forward to by modeling—and teaching them—how to balance life's responsibilities and fun.

Thankfully, we don't have to live miserable lives just because we're grown-ups. Sure, we have a lot of responsibilities. Problems come that require solutions. Sometimes circumstances outside of our control collide with our lives, and we are left to pick up the pieces.

But even so, there is joy and happiness to be had—if we are willing to look for them. There is joy from God's Spirit within us and happiness from the blessings in our lives around us. Ironically, some of my fellow Christian sisters are the unhappiest women I know. They beg God to help them happily bear things He never intended them to live with in the first place.

You do not have to live in misery. There is a beautiful ebb and flow as our supernatural faith intersects with our natural lives. If we believed our happiness was completely God's responsibility, we would act unwisely, refusing to take personal responsibility and not minding the parts of our lives that are under our control.

> There is a beautiful ebb and flow as our supernatural faith intersects with our natural lives.

Imagine having a job you hate, that makes you dread waking up every morning. You have the "scaries" every Sunday night even thinking about going to work. You get tension headaches, your hair is falling out, and you have a perpetually upset stomach due to stress. This job is making your life miserable.

At this point there are two well-trodden paths you could take. One, you could pray every day for God to help you handle it, for grace for yourself, the ability to bear your toxic boss, and for Him to deliver you from your worldly anxiety and worries. Two, you could quit and get a new job. It might not feel easy; in fact, it might be scary and require complete reliance on God in the moment, but it doesn't have to be complicated. Sometimes we spend months or years begging God to deliver us from something we can remedy easily. Sometimes we just need to act.

On the flip side, if we act as if our happiness and joy are all up to us, we become anxious, neurotic, stressed, and worn out. We intuitively know we aren't in control of the universe even if we do everything "right." Which, of course, is impossible in the first place.

We often swing between these two extremes. We run ourselves into the ground without trusting God or asking for wisdom for our current situation. Or we let chaos unfold around us, do very little to change, and then beg God to rescue us.

It reminds me of another story you may have heard before.[1]

THE STORY OF THE DROWNING WOMAN

There once was a woman who lived in a big house on a riverbank. One fateful day a torrential downpour hit her town, and soon the river started flooding. Warnings and alerts to evacuate or get to high ground went out to everyone who lived nearby.

The woman was scared to drive in such weather, so she sat on her front porch to watch the storm unfold. As a large van drove by, the driver slowed down. He rolled down the window, honked the horn, and yelled, "You're not safe here! Jump in. We don't have much time!"

The woman—though admittedly afraid—said to the driver, "No, thanks. The Bible says when I go through rivers of difficulty, I will not drown. I have faith that God will take care of me and the flood won't overwhelm me."

The driver shook his head and drove off. The water kept rising.

Pretty soon the house's first floor was flooded, so the woman had to go to the second floor. She stood on her balcony surveying the scene. She saw a boat making the rounds, and it started toward her. The man steering the vessel came close and yelled through the wind, "Get onboard. Let us help get you out of here. It's not worth the risk."

"I'm not worried about anything," said the woman, "because I pray about everything. I have faith that God's grace is sufficient, that I was made for such a time as this, and that everything happens for a reason. It will all be okay. God will take care of me, and I'll be fine."

The man piloting the boat gave her a confused look, shrugged, and steered toward the next house. The water kept rising.

Eventually the woman had to climb on her roof, the last part of her home not submerged. A rescue helicopter doing a flyover saw her there. The pilot hovered above her, dropped a ladder, and shouted through a megaphone, "We have room for one more!" The woman shook her head, and the pilot called out, "The flood is still rising, and you'll probably drown if you don't climb this ladder and come with us. Let us help you!"

"Don't worry about me," the woman shouted. "My help comes from the Lord! He will never leave me nor forsake me!"

The helicopter flew away. The water continued to rise, and eventually the woman drowned.

At the pearly gates the woman said to God in frustration, "I had a lot of faith in You, but You let me die!"

To that God replied, "I sent you a car, a boat, and then a helicopter. What more did you want?"

While in jest, this fable isn't intended to make fun of the woman who drowned. Of course, we should call out to God when we're in distress. But we also shouldn't resign ourselves to mental, physical, spiritual, or emotional death by inaction or the refusal to accept help. So what does that look like in our lives?

TRUST IN GOD AND ACT WITH WISDOM

You and I need both an enduring faith stronger than our circumstances and the good sense to make wise choices. A healthy blend of the supernatural and the natural. Or supernaturally natural, if you will. Not just praying that God will rescue you, but praying for God to reveal a new path before you. Not just berating yourself for feeling anxious, but figuring out what aspects of your life are causing anxiety and, if possible, eliminating them—or if that isn't feasible, finding clever solutions to minimize the stress. Recognize that having limits and keeping boundaries do not make you selfish, but human. Which of the following changes to your thinking or actions could bring the most peace and order to your life?

- Learn to sift out and reject cultural messages or attitudes that damage your mental, emotional, or spiritual health. Replace those with thoughts that are noble, lovely, and admirable (see Philippians 4:8).
- Stop believing that either the children or the adults in your home get the short end of the stick and start searching for win-win solutions.
- Understand that a lack of rules doesn't make you a positive parent and that too many rules (not attached to your boundaries or values) may wear you out.

- Pay attention when you find yourself trying to live up to impossible standards that set you up to fail. Instead develop standards based on Scripture, your true values, and what's realistic in this stage of your life.
- Don't be afraid to be vulnerable with trustworthy friends, and nurture that support as if your life depends on it. One day it may.
- Quit viewing your emotions as your enemy and instead view them as warning bells to help you dig deeper into what's happening inside your spirit, soul, and body.
- Cultivate the habit of taking good care of the one body God gave you—the one you need for this earthly life—without guilt.
- Create a home environment that brings peace to your family and serves as a haven from the chaotic outside world.
- Be relentless in taking responsibility for your own life and everything under your control (but not those things outside of it). This is a quick path away from powerlessness.

The sixteenth-century theologian Ignatius of Loyola put it like this:

I consider it an error to trust and hope in any means or efforts in themselves alone; nor do I consider it a safe path to trust the whole matter to God our Lord without desiring to help myself by what he has given me; so that it seems to me in our Lord that I ought to make use of both parts, desiring in all things his greater praise and glory, and nothing else.[2]

In other words, pray as if everything depends on God but don't neglect the common sense He gave you.

Know that apart from God you cannot find true peace in yourself or in your efforts, but you can work to rid your life of the chaos, strife, and disorder that block that peace.

Trust in God. And learn to pedal with the wind, not against it.

DISCOVER YOUR BOUNDARY MARKERS

1. I am more likely to rely on my own abilities and plow ahead than to trust God and ask for His wisdom in these situations:

2. I regularly beg God to rescue me from the following areas in which I feel too overwhelmed to act:

PUT A FLAG ON THEM!

1. I no longer want to depend only on my own strength when it comes to _____

   _____.

2. Knowing that God has promised to give me the wisdom and strength I need to deal with this difficult situation,

   _____,

   I will pray and then take one small step, _____

   _____, to move forward.

STRUCTURES, RULES, OR ROUTINES TO PROTECT YOUR BOUNDARIES

Brainstorm some ways you can both work hard and seek after God's wisdom and help in difficult areas of life. How can you invite God into the process? What other friends might you invite to come alongside and help you?

As you come to the end of the book, list two to three new structures, rules, or routines from chapters 5–13 that you most want to begin or continue, knowing they are attainable and will ultimately bring you (and your family) peace, contentment, and joy.

1.

2.

3.

I consider it an error to trust and hope in any means
or efforts in themselves alone; nor do I consider it a
safe path to trust the whole matter to God our Lord
without desiring to help myself by what he has given
me; so that it seems to me in our Lord that I ought
to make use of both parts, desiring in all things his
greater praise and glory, and nothing else.

Ignatius of Loyola

Notes

CHAPTER 1: HAPPY-GO-LUCKY . . . OR NOT

1. Robert Preidt, "Depression Striking More Young People Than Ever," WebMD, May 11, 2018, copyright © 2013–2018 HealthDay, https://www.webmd.com/depression/news/20180511/depression-striking-more-young-people-than-ever. See also Alexis E. Carrington, MD, "Anxiety, Depression Increasing among Mothers during the COVID-19 Pandemic," ABC News, July 4, 2020, https://abcnews.go.com/Health/anxiety-depression-increasing-mothers-covid-19-pandemic/story?id=71605965.
2. Matthew 6:27

CHAPTER 2: SENDING THE WRONG MESSAGE

1. Hillary Morgan Ferrer, general ed., *Mama Bear Apologetics: Empowering Your Kids to Challenge Cultural Lies* (Eugene, OR: Harvest House, 2019), 54.

CHAPTER 3: HARD STOP: LIMITS, BOUNDARIES, AND PREFERENCES

1. For more information, see https://www.languageoflistening.com/.
2. Lee Brice, "Love Like Crazy," on Lee Brice, Curb Records, 2010.

CHAPTER 4: TRANSFORMING LOSING SITUATIONS INTO WIN-WIN SOLUTIONS

1. Lexico, s.v., "selfish," accessed September 7, 2021, https://www.lexico.com/en/definition/selfish.

CHAPTER 5: MINDING YOUR OWN RULES

1. Camilla Miller, Keeping Your Cool Parenting, https://keepingyourcoolparenting.com/about/.

CHAPTER 7: MINDING YOUR OWN FRIENDS

1. Kelly A. Turner, *Radical Remission: Surviving Cancer against All Odds* (San Francisco: HarperOne, 2015); Chris Wark, *Chris Beat Cancer: A Comprehensive Plan for Healing Naturally* (Carlsbad, CA: Hay House, 2018).
2. See "The Dangers of Present but Absent Parenting" at https://amotherfarfromhome.com/present-but-absent-parent/ and "The Habit Every Mom Starts When Nursing—but Wishes She Hadn't," https://amotherfarfromhome.com/reliance-smart-phone/.
3. Joshua 24:15 and 1 Timothy 6:6

CHAPTER 8: MINDING YOUR OWN EMOTIONS

1. Fulvio D'Acquisto, "Affective Immunology: Where Emotions and the Immune Response Converge," *Dialogues in Clinical Neuroscience* 19, no. 1 (March 2017): 9–19, https://www.ncbi.nlm.nih.gov/pmc/articles/PMC5442367/;
   Suzanne C. Segerstrom and Gregory E. Miller, "Psychological Stress and the Human Immune System: A Meta-Analytic Study of 30 Years of Inquiry," *Psychological Bulletin* 130, no. 4 (July 2004): 601–630, https://www.ncbi.nlm.nih.gov/pmc/articles/PMC1361287/.
2. *It Didn't Start with You* by Mark Wolynn (New York: Penguin, 2016) is a great book on this topic that explores how unresolved emotions can even be passed down to our children.
3. Julie Fraga, "Therapy for Every Budget: How to Access It," Healthline, February 21, 2022, https://www.healthline.com/health/therapy-for-every-budget#Introduction-to-affordable-therapy.

CHAPTER 9: MINDING YOUR OWN DAILY CARE

1. Francesco P. Cappuccio, et al., "Sleep Duration and All-Cause Mortality: A Systematic Review and Meta-Analysis of Prospective Studies," *Sleep* 33, no. 5 (May 1, 2010): 585–592, https://www.ncbi.nlm.nih.gov/pmc/articles/PMC2864873/.

CHAPTER 10: MINDING YOUR OWN RESPONSIBILITIES

1. Chris Wark, *Beat Cancer Daily: 365 Days of Inspiration, Encouragement, and Action Steps to Survive and Thrive* (Carlsbad, CA: Hay House, 2020), Day 3.
2. "The Real Reason Moms Never Have Enough Time (Hint: It's Not Because They Waste It)," https://amotherfarfromhome.com/moms-dont-have-time/.

CHAPTER 11: MINDING YOUR OWN HOME

1. Alexander Harris, "U.S. Self-Storage Industry Statistics," The SpareFoot Storage Beat, updated January 27, 2021, https://www.sparefoot.com/self -storage/news/1432-self-storage-industry-statistics/.

2. University of Minnesota, "Involving Children in Household Tasks: Is It Worth the Effort?" September 2002, https://ghk.h-cdn.co/assets/cm/15 /12/55071e0298a05_-_Involving-children-in-household-tasks-U-of-M.pdf.

CHAPTER 12: MINDING YOUR OWN LIFE

1. This quote is attributed to H. Jackson Brown Jr., author of *Life's Little Instruction Book* (Thomas Nelson, 2000).

2. This is a paraphrase of the fable told in Timothy Ferriss's, *The 4-Hour Workweek: Escape 9–5, Live Anywhere, and Join the New Rich* (New York: Crown Publishers, 2007), 252–253.

CHAPTER 13: YOUR TRUE NORTH

1. A version of this story appears in many places, including on Michael Hartzell's blog: "The Story about a Jeep, a Boat, and a Helicopter," https:// www.michaelhartzell.com/blog/the-story-about-a-jeep-a-boat-and-a -helicopter.

2. Trent Horn, "St. Ignatius Said What?" Catholic Answers, July 31, 2019, https://www.catholic.com/magazine/online-edition/st-ignatius-said-what?

About the Author

Rachel Norman is a mother, an authorized Language of Listening® parent coach, and a baby and toddler sleep consultant. She is also the founder of A Mother Far from Home, an online community dedicated to helping young mothers create peaceful and enjoyable lives for their families. Her website focuses on family and personal routines, boundaries, healthy sleep habits, and emotional and mental well-being for both parents and children.

Before founding A Mother Far from Home in 2012, Rachel got her bachelor's degree in criminology and law and her master's degree in public administration. Upon graduation, she completed a TESOL (Teaching English as a Second Language) certificate and lived in Italy for a couple of years, where she became fluent in Italian. She then attended a discipleship program in England, where she met her husband, and they spent the next few years living in Scotland and Australia as they grew their family.

Having five babies in five years gave her a passion for family life, which inspired the creation of her online business. Today, she has more than 100,000 followers on social media and 130,000-plus subscribers to her weekly parenting newsletter. She also continues to encourage more than a million mothers a year on her website.

Rachel resides in DeFuniak Springs, Florida, with her husband, Matthew, and their five young children. She loves the beach, boating, traveling, reading, and being with her family.